17-5

GRANDPARENTING TODAY'S TEENS

Offer your grandkids what no one else can.

Mark Gregston

FIRST EDITION

ISBN: 978-1-946466-54-9

Library of Congress Control Number: 2018956383

Published by

P.O. Box 2839, Apopka, FL 32704

In partnership with

Printed in the United States of America

Dedication

To Jan, my wife, and the greatest grandmother I know.
Who would have ever thought that a first date in ninth grade to
see a Led Zeppelin concert, would one day lead to us being
grandparents together forty-seven years later to four wonderful
grandchildren, Maile, Macie, Chase, and Carter.

Acknowledgments

A special thank you to the following folks who have influenced the writing of this book.

To David Muth, Dave Tillack, and Smith Brookhart for providing so many lessons that I learned from you and for showing me how to do this *legacy thing* right. Rest in peace, dear friends.

To Heartlight Ministries and all the staff who provide the perfect laboratory for me to learn about grandparents, parents, and teens. A special thanks to the board of directors, Blake and Melissa Nelson, John and Amy Hull, Jonathan and Jillian Greifenkamp, Andy and Lisa Deer, and Mike and Carol Barry for your friendship and help with making Heartlight a wonderful place for families and teens.

To the Heartlight Ministries Foundation for fulfilling the mission to offer help and hope to a broken world. A special thanks to the board of directors, Bill and Susanne Walsh, Roger and Lori Kemp, Jerry and Leanne Heuer, George and Livia Dunklin, Alan and Belinda Carter, and Lee and Jodie Caple for your continued and much appreciated support.

To Diamond Resort's Cabo Azul for providing the best place to gather thoughts and write about grandparenting.

To Bill and Gloria Gaither. This was your idea and how thankful I am for your suggestion to reach out to grandparents everywhere.

To Roger Kemp & Co., Wayne Shepherd, Joe Carlson, KT Losie,

and Sam Sheeley for making our *mass communicatin'* a haven of hope and a place of blessing for so many parents.

And of course, Jan, whom I get to figure this parenting and grandparenting out with. I wish I had had a grandmother like you are to our kid's kids.

Table of Contents

Foreword 9

Introduction 13

PART I — YOUR ROLE

Chapter 1   You Have a Place in Their Lives
Even if You're Old as Dirt 21

Chapter 2   Don't Save the Best for Last 27

Chapter 3   How to Give Big-Picture Perspective
to Your Grandchild's World 35

Chapter 4   A Grandparent's Greatest Challenge...............43

PART II — YOUR PRESENCE

Chapter 5   Why Gray Hair Works to Your Benefit 55

Chapter 6   Changing Gears When You're Almost Out of Gas 63

Chapter 7   Maintaining Your Relationship
in a Not-So-Relational Culture 77

Chapter 8   Being a Superhero When Their Lives Suck 85

Chapter 9   How a Place of Retreat Becomes a Haven of Rest 91

Chapter 10   Touching Their Hearts When Their Behavior
Hurts Your Heart 101

Chapter 11   When Health Gets in the Way 111

PART III — YOUR LIFE'S WORDS

Chapter 12   Giving Your Grandkids What They Want 121
Chapter 13   Since Nagging and Lecturing Don't Work,
             Try Something Different! 137
Chapter 14   Not Every Argument Needs to be Argued....................149
Chapter 15   Quit Correcting and Start Connecting........................157

PART IV — YOUR LIFE'S ACTIONS

Chapter 16   Complaining Ruins Relationships;
             Gratefulness Draws Them In 167
Chapter 17   Can Everyone Just Laugh a Little? 175
Chapter 18   You're Kidding Me. This is Important? 183
Chapter 19   Won't Somebody Just Listen! 193
Chapter 20   Play it Smart; They're Watching...............203
Chapter 21   A Legacy of Relationship............................211

PART V — YOUR LEGACY

Chapter 22   Supporting Your Grandkid's Parents...........217
Chapter 23   Making Memories Before You Lose Yours..................229
Chapter 24   Transferring What You Believe to be Important..........239
Chapter 25   When Life Gives You a Mulligan:
             A Chance to Make it Right............................249

End Notes..259
About the Author..260

Foreword

In this, his newest book, Mark Gregston addresses a huge vacuum in family help—grandparenting. For over forty years Mark and his wife Jan have been working with teenagers who are having a hard time navigating the rocky road of adolescence. As they state it: "Our goal is to restore what is broken, redeem what is lost, and defend the defenseless." They have helped an army of parents rescue their kids.

Few authors and counselors have addressed the issues of one of the greatest resources for rescuing and providing stability for kids at the most precarious junctures of their journeys—grandparents. Oh, there are books on how cute grandkids are and delightful books giving ideas for spending time with grandkids. But we grandparents need real, serious help solving knotty problems, tackling issues that threaten our families, and figuring out how to leave our grandchildren with deep convictions and strong character that instill principles for living in their own kids long after we are gone.

Soon after 1990, Irene Endicott, a pioneer in the area of grandparenting, went to the US Census Bureau to find out how many grandparents there were in America. There were no such statistics. The question had never been asked on the Census form. The closest was a question that asked a person what his/her relationship was to the others living in their home. Even AARP, the powerful national lobbying organization for older people didn't know the number of grandparents in the United States.

Moreover, although many grandparents were raising their grandkids because of dysfunction in the middle generation, they could not apply or be granted foster parent status or subsidies, though many were supporting grandkids on limited incomes. Even at the publication of her first book *Grandparenting Redefined* in 1992, Endicott found that 5% of American families consisted of a grandparent raising a grandchild and that "one-third of initial child abuse calls received by children and youth agencies end[ed] with informal arrangements with relatives— mostly grandparents." (Endicott, p. 13)

Now, twenty-five years later, much has changed and not for the better. More families are in crisis, and more young people need grandparents than ever before.

The image of a gray-haired woman in a print dress and a man in bib overalls rocking on the porch is a long-gone fantasy. Most *grandmas* I know are zipping around on the mopeds they hauled to Florida on the back or their oversized motor homes. Even more, grandparents are themselves on the second and third marriages and share an assortment of step-grandchildren who don't remember a home place where they *can always go home to grandma.*

I'm just saying that grandkids and grandparents need real help and intelligent wisdom in these tumultuous days. How do we help without hovering? How do we enfold without enabling? How do we stay involved without intimidating? And how do we leave our kids and grandkids a legacy that *will not rust* and *where thieves cannot break in and steal*? How can we instill in the generations that follow a hunger for soul food that satisfies an unquenchable thirst for Living Water?

Bless Mark Gregston for wading into the deep waters of need with his pant legs rolled up and his sleeves too! Bless him for taking on us grandparents and our misconceptions of modern teenagers and for helping us see these kids with more potential and dearer hearts than we ever dreamed. And bless him for giving us the confidence to know that we can make an eternal difference in these less-than optimistic times.

Bill and Gloria Gaither

Introduction

I didn't really know any of my grandparents. They were distant and old. One set lived in the booming metropolis of Ryan, Oklahoma, and the other in the small northern Kansas town of Concordia. By the time I was twelve, they were all in bad shape. They didn't seem to care much about my brother, sister, and me. Their focus just wasn't on grandkids.

I knew my dad's dad as one who was in and out of a nursing home. I remember watching him take out his teeth at dinner and eat bread that was soaked in milk. I don't remember him ever saying a word to me. There was never a connection.

My dad's mom was a quiet lady. She never said much of anything, but she laughed a lot. She traveled into the Oklahoma Territory in a covered wagon and lived in a log cabin in her adolescent years. Her dad had a huge mustache. She was not much for conversation, but she loved to make chocolate cake. Every time I see a chocolate cake, I think of my paternal grandma. And when I saw my grandma, I'd think of her chocolate cake…and not much else.

The only thing I can remember about my mom's dad was his views of anyone who wasn't white and let's just say his views don't bear repeating. He also didn't have time for us, so we never made time for him.

My mom's mom was frail and somewhat critical in spirit. I never saw her laugh, never enjoyed being with her and my grandpa, and couldn't wait to drive away from that little north Kansas town whenever we were there.

You now know the total of all my memories of my grandparents. Isn't that sad? In just five small paragraphs, you know everything about the roles my grandparents played in my life (or didn't play is more like it). It's not that I hated them. I just wasn't sure I loved them, as it's hard to love someone with whom you have no relationship. There were no values or morals transferred. There were no stories of family traditions of fun times together. Never a mention of what they believed or hoped for. No instruction. No wisdom shared. And, sadly, no love lost when each passed away.

So when my daughter told me when I was forty-six that I was going to be a grandfather, it scared me to death. I had no idea what I was supposed to do or what this grandparenting thing was supposed to look like. My examples were negligible and negative and hardly a type of grandparenting I wanted to emulate.

But I was excited. Deep down, I knew a new adventure was about to unfold. I couldn't wait.

My first thought upon hearing, "You're going to be a grandpa!" was, *I can't be that old.* I was somewhat hesitant to admit to others that I was going to become one. I never thought the young lady I started dating in the ninth grade and married six years later would end up being a grandparent with me. Did that mean I was going to be sleeping with a *grandma* the rest of my days? The whole concept of this new role petrified me. I even remember telling my daughter, "I'm probably not going to do well with this grandchild until they reach their teens…so don't expect much."

As I waited with anticipation outside my daughter's birthing room, I wondered what this grandpa thing was going to be. Then I heard this little six-pound, eight-ounce newborn cry seconds after my granddaughter was born, and my life changed forever. It was a heart change that mellowed this type-A personality, driven fellow into a golden retriever puppy dog. I couldn't quit crying. I couldn't take enough photographs.

The first time I actually held my granddaughter, I wondered if my grandparents ever held me when I was born. I wondered if they felt the same thing the first time they saw me. I don't think they did. I determined right then to *do it differently.* I wanted to have a relationship with my grandkids. I wanted to impact each one of their lives. I wanted to be involved. I did not want to be remembered as someone who ate milk-soaked bread and never spoke, one who made racist comments, one who was critical all the time, or one who just made a great chocolate cake.

I wanted, and still want, to leave a legacy—something that makes a profound difference in the lives of my grandkids. I want to influence them in the best possible ways, ways I know that only I can. Of all the grandparents and all the grandkids in the world, mine were chosen for me. I take that seriously. It is an honor and a privilege. I want to leave them a legacy of hope.

If that legacy is to be, it can only happen through a special relationship that I have to develop and work on continually. I have to seek new ways to offer my wisdom and love gathered through the years, to affect my grandchildren in a way that is so much more than what I observed grandparenting to be. I never read a grandparenting manual, but I have a natural longing to connect with the kids of my kids. I want my grandkids to know they are just as important in my life and to our family as my own kids.

I grew up with the notion that grandparents were people you saw occasionally, who retired at sixty-five and were dead by seventy, people who exerted little or no influence on their grandkids or made any real impact on them. I am determined to be a different kind of grandparent than that.

I'm sure many of you have or had grandparents who made a mark on your life. And I'm sure that many had grandparents just like mine. In either case, chances are good you'll live to be a lot older than your parents did, and you'll have an opportunity to leave a bigger mark on the life of your grandkids. Medicine, healthy eating, and exercise are not collaborating to give you immortality on this earth. That's impossible. But the progress made in each of these areas is allowing us to remain on this planet a little bit longer. I think we can use that time to offer a younger generation the help it needs to counter the effects this culture is having (and always has had) on today's adolescents.

I believe this: God is keeping you around a little longer so you can have influence, impact, and a marked impression on the lives of your grandkids. That's the legacy I mentioned earlier.

If you're going to be involved in the lives of your grandchildren and desperately want to make a mark on their lives, then you have to work hard to keep the relationship active and *up-to-date*. You have to understand their world so your words, guidance, and wisdom can have their full effect on their lives. You have to change with the times, figuring out what's new in their lives (even if that makes you feel like an antique). You have to make adjustments. Pursue their hearts on their terms. Learn to bite your tongue. Determine when to speak, when *not* to share your opinion, and how to make yourself available in their lives so they feel a sense of rest in your presence.

I know, because I've spent the last forty years watching grandparents get involved in the lives of their grandkids. We have had over three thousand kids live us through the years at Heartlight, our residential counseling center for struggling teens. I've seen the impact many grandparents have had, and an equal number of *failures to connect* from other grandparents. Certain traits connect grandkids to grandparents, and there are behaviors that prevent positive, impactful relationships from ever happening.

It's not as much about what you do as it is creating an atmosphere where relationships can grow. It's about adapting to their world where they can learn more about who you are.

Your grandkids need you now more than ever, especially in their teen years. God has a plan to use you as a messenger of timeless truth in their ever-changing world. Your position is unique. Your relationship is paramount. Pursue it well. Make the most of the years you have to invest in the lives of your grandkids. I hope this book helps you do exactly that!

PART I — YOUR ROLE

Chapter 1

You Have a Place in Their Lives Even if You're Old as Dirt

Grandchildren are the crown of old men.
Proverbs 17:6 (NASB)

It was a hot, humid day in East Texas—one of those burning, scorching days where Texans wish they were somewhere a thousand miles north of where they live. It was so hot that the only places to battle the oppressive heat was inside with the air conditioning cranked up, outside in the swimming pool, or playing in the sprinkler in your front yard.

Maile, my first granddaughter, opted for the sprinkler. She was nineteen months old and spending the day with Mamaw (my wife Jan), a day meant for fun and hanging out. Maile wanted to try out the new turtle-shaped water sprinkler, which was a perfect antidote to the lingering heat on this Texas afternoon.

I was driving home from work and turned into our driveway, the hundred-yard road that leads to our home. As soon as I pulled in, I could see Jan in the front yard. The turtle sprayed cool water. Maile stood in the front yard butt-naked, laughing, and frolicking innocently through the spraying fountain of water.

As I drove up, Maile spotted me and immediately started sprinting toward me. Seeing her, I stopped my truck and got out to hear her screaming excitedly at the top of her lungs, "Poppa! Poppa!" Her little arms waved, and her little legs toddled toward me as fast as they could.

I stood there, watching her run toward me, and all of a sudden, everything went into slow motion. It was as if my brain wanted to stop and take it all in, or perhaps my heart just wanted to savor the moment. The innocence of that simple moment, watching this tiny little girl in nothing but her shoes, so excited to see her Poppa, immediately brought tears to my eyes and such joy to my heart. I laughed and cried at the same time. And I knew…I mean, I *knew* from the bottom of my heart that I had a place in hers.

She jumped into my arms. I stood there, holding this soaking wet, twenty-pound little girl as she hugged my neck, begging me to play in the sprinkler with her. Later, Jan told me she had never seen me smile as big as I did that day. I joked with my wife that she would see me smile like that more often if she greeted me like Maile did every time I arrived home. (Her response was something to the effect of "Don't count on it.")

That day revealed how special my relationship with my granddaughter was, and continues to be, as is my relationship with all my grandchildren. I promised myself I would work hard and diligently to keep it that way.

That promise was pretty easy to keep the first twelve years of Maile's life. During that period, I could do no wrong. When your kids first have kids, you *ooh* and *ahh* over that new baby and lavish them with gifts. The sheer cuteness factor of the child keeps grandparents attached and connected. Matter of fact, grandparents might even score a coffee mug that says, "World's Greatest Grandpa" (or Grandma) or a T-shirt that states "Grandpa: the Man, the Myth, the Legend," or "SuperGrandma" during your grandkids elementary school years.

Once Maile reached middle school, keeping our relationship special became a little harder than I anticipated. The competition for time with her increased, and I realized if I didn't remain engaged, the bond I committed to maintaining and impact I promised to make would soon be casualties of adolescent interests taking her to *greener pastures*.

As your grandkids get a little older, their social circles grow as well. The amount of time they have for you becomes scarcer as years pass. As they enter their teen years, the time with grandparents gets pushed to the side. Other interests try to take your place during your grandchildren's adolescent stage.

Before you know it, they're off to college, and the distance in space and time grows even larger. Then they get married, and the time slot once reserved for grandparents shrinks even further. Once your grandchildren have kids, just about the only time left to spend with this *crown of old men* is holidays, an occasional picture for the books (or for social media in this day and age), or a quick catch-up call on the phone.

I'm sure you've attended many funerals of grandparents where the only interactions with the grandkids that were mentioned took place thirty or forty years ago. Eulogies that only talk about the distant past reflect a disconnect somewhere. A disconnect I'm sure grandparents never wanted or intended. Somewhere and somehow, in the process of getting older, grandparents find they have more time on their hands just when their grandchildren's schedules get fuller and fuller. A grandparent's desire to stay engaged and involved in the lives of grandkids gets edged out and lost as calendars fill with the activities that come with their own kids and responsibilities.

It's important to remember your role in their lives is still vital. You have a place in their lives, but you have to make it happen. You have to be the one who pursues the relationship during the teen years because the time crunch and overabundance of choices in their lives will eliminate you before you even recognize the beginning of the *great divide*. And if you don't pursue them during this time of their lives, I fear it will be hard to recover real relationship in your later years.

I think teens have a tough time making good choices. Not because they necessarily lack the skills to choose, but because there are so many options it's just hard for them to be selective and pick what will truly satisfy.

I don't know about you, but the number of choices for me in many cases frustrates me. And I'm a quick decision maker. I don't want to read twenty pages of menu options at a restaurant. I don't like selecting the right cheese out of hundreds of cheeses on the grocery store shelf.

You want your relationship to be one they value and see the significance in embracing.

I don't enjoy finding the right program if I have to search through hundreds of channels on the television. Many times, I order any old food just to get it over with. I select a type of cheese because I'm tired of looking. Or I settle on some TV program because I can't find what I was looking for, or forget in the process of pushing buttons on the remote. We often default to what is the most easily available.

Amidst all the choices your grandkids have in their lives, you can help them make spending time with you an easy decision. I know you don't want them to choose you because they have to; you want them to choose you because of what your relationship has to offer. You want your relationship to be one they value and see the significance in embracing.

So make it an easy choice for them.

That's really what this book is all about. Understanding the world your grandkids live in and figuring out how to be part of it. Period. Common sense tells how different our grandkids' world is than the one we grew up in. Our crucial and necessary challenge is to figure out how to remain relevant and beneficial in the lives of those *special relationships* that changed our world from the moment they entered it.

You maintained those relationships during their earlier years, but it's a whole new ballgame during their teen years. That's when they need you the most. Make sure it's not a time when they see you the least. Your habits of engagement have got to change. You can't keep correcting their mistakes. You're going to have to accept some things in their lives that weren't acceptable in yours. Your communication style has got to change with their maturing need to hear a different message that pertains to *their* stage in life. You've got to allow your grandkids to become young men and women, to become husbands and wives, and eventually moms and dads and treat them as such. Lord willing, one day they'll even be grandmas and grandpas. And your legacy can continue through them into their own grandchildren.

There is a great need for a connection with you. It's a lifelong need, where you become a safe place, a place where you listen more than you speak, encourage more than you correct, and laugh more often with them than you get upset by their actions. They may not know it, but your presence in their lives is important. As long as health allows and the ability to connect remains, your grandkids need you in their lives.

Don't think a yearly vacation together is enough to keep the relational fires burning between you and your grandchild, any more than a once-a-year connection with friends maintains real relationships. It's not where you vacation, it's how you get there that makes the difference. Kind words, interest in their world, asking what they think, and humble offers to help any way you can all year long make that annual vacation a memory builder and unforgettable experience.

Here's my point: You've got to make the relationship happen. Your grandchild is busy growing up, becoming social, maturing, and trying out independence in the teen years. All that growth and maturity tries to push grandparents right out of the picture. Don't let it.

You have a choice to make. You can allow your relationship to fade away by the teen years and beyond, or you can embrace the role God placed you in for a purpose. All grandparents can

> They may not know it, but your presence in their lives is important.

have a positive influence on kids, in a day and age where influential relationships are in short supply and low demand.

Here's another piece of advice: Do it now. Time is flying by and we'll be gone before we know it.

I don't want to go and have my kids or grandkids shed tears over a sense of regret that ol' Grandpa *used to be involved* in the life of his family. I want them to cry tears of joy that Poppa *has been involved* in every stage of their lives. Because you're reading this book, I know you feel the same.

You have an important role in their lives. And they desperately need you. How you engage, make changes, and approach your grandkids during their teen years will determine if you can make your role and their need for you come together to fulfill all your lives.

Chapter 2

Don't Save the Best for Last

For where your treasure is, there your heart will be also.
Luke 12:34 (KJV)

During the last ten years of my mom's life, she always told me how fast time flies and how it flies even faster with each passing day. Now that I'm in my sixties, I can comprehend what she was trying to tell me. Why it seems like I'm filling thirty-day prescriptions every other day. Sixty seconds seems like thirty. It feels like Christmas is every other month and my teeth are getting cleaned every other week. Life is sure speeding up.

Before you know it, that ol' body of yours will begin to wither, age will remind you of your limitations, and you'll be a number you never thought possible, wondering *where did all the time go?* The relentless marching on of the aging process will come at you through medical issues, gray hair, wrinkles, failing eyesight, droopy skin, and loss of hearing. Embracing the frailty of life and the promise of it one day ending can change who you are, how you are perceived, and the impact you will have on others.

Everything you own will one day be given away. All your accumulations, money, collections, clothes, memorabilia—all of it— will be given away to family and friends, if not sold off to complete strangers. Comforting thought, isn't it?

After my mom died, we moved my dad into a retirement village because, as he put it, "The house is pretty quiet." We could all tell that the silence was taking a toll on him and would eventually drive him crazy. As we moved him into his new place, we moved out all the belongings he and my mom had acquired throughout their sixty-two years of marriage. I'm not sure why, but my dad stated all he needed to move to his new place was a couple of pieces of furniture, his clothes, his computer, and a pot to fix food in. Perhaps the loss of a spouse makes you realize how frivolous things are. He was reeling from his own grief and the prospect of now living life on his own in a new place with strangers around him. Who cared about doilies and knickknacks?

My siblings and I talked about what we each wanted from my parents' lifelong collection of belongings. Surprisingly, we didn't want much. Still, the thought of just giving it all away or selling it to others felt tough to process. I, too, grieved the loss of my mom and the change that was happening within our family now that she was gone.

I rented a trailer and brought a ton of stuff home to Texas, where a few months later we had a garage sale and gave away much of my mom's history to people she never knew, families she never met, and strangers from countries she never visited. Then it hit me; the collection of all the stuff in our lives is just that—*stuff*.

I asked my kids what they wanted of mine when I died. My daughter couldn't think of anything. My son told me he wanted my guns and a few pairs of my boots. I remember saying, *"That's it? That's all you want? Just those things?"*

He answered, "Yep, that's about it."

In 1974, I lost all my belongings to a tornado in Tulsa, OK. That event taught me about the value of things. My son's comments about what he wanted from my belongings showed me what holds true value. It isn't all the *stuff* I've been collecting all my life, any more than what my mom gathered during hers.

The most valuable things in life aren't things at all. They're the relationships people form during their time on earth. The pursuit of things (stuff) is frivolous; the pursuit of relationships is fundamental to God's plan for us all. I believe God desires us to invest our time, our resources, and our efforts in relationships.

So here's my first piece of advice in this chapter: Give it away. Give your time, your resources, and your efforts to those around you. In particular, give to your grandkids while they have the time to appreciate it and you have your health to enjoy the giving.

> I believe God desires us to invest our time, our resources, and our efforts in relationships.

Now, I'm one who believes in taking care of yourself financially. I'm a finance guy from the University of Tulsa who embraces what John Wesley stated a couple of centuries ago, that one should, "Earn all you can, save all you can, give all you can."

I'm a believer in financial security, especially as one enters retirement. But I'm all about sharing as well, and there is nothing more rewarding or more impactful than sharing with your family.

Here's a proverb for all you grandparents.

A good person leaves an inheritance for their children's children. (Proverbs 13:22)

I'm convinced of this. And I'm convinced this verse isn't just talking about leaving money, if it's talking about that at all. It's about leaving a legacy, an heirloom, a tradition, and a heritage—something that lasts in the souls of your grandkids.

If you've picked up by now that I think your grandkids' teen years are the time when you can have the greatest influence when they need it the most, you are hearing me correctly. You can leave a valuable inheritance while you are still alive, in the form of memorable events that are magnificent and meaningful. I encourage you to look for opportunities to experience life together with your grandkids, especially during the teen years. Find experiences that will give you memories to share, photos to post, opportunities to have life-on-life involvement, times of laughter together, and chances to build deeper relationships through common activities.

It's been said that the moods of a lifetime are found in the all-but-forgotten experiences of adolescence. I know this to be true after listening to thousands of teens share the unforgettable experiences that shaped their lives and determined their destinies.

Many times I wondered what it would have been like to have a heart full of memories of experiences with my parents and grandparents. I've speculated at what I could have done earlier in my life if someone had given me five thousand dollars when I got married and how that would have helped in so many ways. I've pondered what it would have been like to have grandparents give me something that was dear to them; something passed on that meant something to them. I've wondered what messages I would have gotten if a grandparent had given me advice, taken the time to help in some fashion, or shown me an example of what it was like to value relationships and how to give.

My grandkids challenge me to think about whether I am doing those very things today. The times I wondered what I would have received have now been transformed into thinking about whether I am giving and changing my grandchildren's world with my time, resources, and efforts. That's how a grandparent leaves a legacy.

Here's my second piece of advice for this chapter: Don't wait. Don't save the best for last. You might just miss it.

David Muth and I met when his daughter came to live with us at Heartlight ten years ago. We hit it off the moment we met. His winsome personality was a joy to be around, and his love for his family was attractive. His common sense was welcome wisdom wrapped in his warm sense of humor. We laughed. We laughed a lot together.

David knew I love wine, and we shared bottles of specialty wines throughout the years whenever we got together. We sent wine to each another on holidays or birthdays. Sitting on my back porch, we figured out the deep, hidden issues of life, God, and the souls of men over glasses of fine wine. We had the kind of deep discussions I don't have with many.

David collected wine and always told me about the bottles he was saving for a special occasion. I'm sure I added a few to his *special occasion* collection, all neatly and precisely tucked away for exclusive times of honor and celebration.

He and his wife Amy served on our board of directors at Heartlight, which sometimes felt like an excuse to get together and catch up on our very different lives. His life was the busy hospital life of an anesthesiologist. Mine was the founder of a ranch for struggling teens.

David called me one afternoon to share that he had just been diagnosed with Parkinson's disease. As he described it, this was the Parkinson's that wasn't the *shaky* kind, but one that, over time, would deteriorate the organs in his body. He shared that most people with his diagnosis didn't live more than five or six years. He was going to have to retire at fifty-two and planned to move to Anna Maria Island, Florida, where he would face the challenges of his remaining years with Parkinson's.

After a couple of years of keeping up over the phone, getting updates on his condition, I decided I needed to spend some time with him at his home in Florida. I committed to doing so every couple of months. I'd travel to see him at the tail end of speaking engagements or make a stopover in Tampa on the way back home.

The first time I got there to see him and Amy, I took him a beautiful three-hundred-dollar bottle of wine (Opus) to be used for a special occasion. He tucked it away in his wine stash. At that point in his Parkinson's journey, we always pulled out bottles not designated for special occasions and enjoyed them over the same deep discussions. We also watched movies and laughed until our bellies hurt.

Over time, Parkinson's took more and more of a toll on my dear friend. On one of my trips to see him, he said, "Let's take out one of those bottles I've been saving for a special occasion and have that tonight." He let me know that he had a 1960 Port, a bottle that was fifty-five years old and was his Cadillac of wines. He spent most of his adult life waiting to drink it. I felt privileged to be the recipient of this special occasion.

His hands had gotten to where he couldn't open the bottle, and he asked me to do the honors. As I opened the bottle and began to pour the wine, we were both quick to notice the wine had gone bad. Basically, it had turned to mush. The look of disappointment on his face is one I will never forget. All the hope he held onto for so many years of enjoying that special bottle of wine was dashed.

Next, he said, "Well, I have a 1968 Bordeaux (French) I've been saving."

I opened it up and much to our surprise, it had gone bad as well.

He continued, "Well, I have a 1974 Barolo I've been saving for a special occasion. Let's open up that one." We did, and much to our shock, it had gone bad as well.

"Well, I have a 1992 Screaming Eagle from Napa I've been saving for a special occasion. Let's give that one a shot." We did, and to our dismay, the same scenario repeated itself. David began to realize that what he had been saving for was all in vain.

After a couple more bottles of wine brought the same ending, I asked David if we could just open the bottle I brought him months ago—that Opus I gave him for a special occasion. He relented, and we both enjoyed.

> Don't save for that *special occasion* because the *special occasion* is today.

That night as I lay awake in David and Amy's guest bedroom, I kept thinking over and over what lesson was to be learned from what just happened. This is what I concluded: Don't save for that *special occasion* because the *special occasion* is today.

The fact that we were both together that day was occasion enough to enjoy the very best. I committed to this. Anytime someone comes to my home, and we share wine, I'm going to pull out the very best and most expensive bottle of wine I have and serve it. I'm not going to wait for any *special occasion* because that *special occasion* is now. This moment.

Catch what I'm saying? Don't wait. Your grandkids need you now.

Time passes way too quickly not to take advantage of the present that is today.

Don't wait until you're no longer busy; that will never happen.

Don't wait until that special occasion; it is happening around you every day.

Don't wait until you can afford it because you can't afford *not* to.

Don't wait until you can find the time; it passes way too quickly.

Don't miss the opportunity during your grandkids' teen years; it will be gone too soon.

You will never be appreciated more or have a greater impact at any other time than the *special occasion* that is before you today.

Chapter 3

How to Give Big-Picture Perspective to Your Grandchild's World

The beginning of wisdom is this: Get wisdom.
Though it cost all you have, get understanding.
Proverbs 4:7

Taylor Swift is one of the best-selling country/pop artists of all time. She is the recipient of ten Grammy Awards, twenty-one Billboard Music Awards, eleven Country Music Association Awards, and countless other awards too many to list. All the accolades meant nothing to my two granddaughters. They were just dying to see this popular artist perform. When they found out T-Swizzle was coming to a venue just a few miles from where we all lived, no one would rest until tickets were secured.

My daughter was charged with purchasing the tickets, which she quickly did just before the concert sold out. The day came, and the five of us set off for the concert; two little girls dressed like Taylor, one mom wanting to please her kids, and two grandparents who love country music and wanted to see this phenomenon named Taylor.

Jan and I have been to quite a few concerts throughout our lives, and the challenge of each ticket purchase is to get as close to the front of the venue as possible or at least reasonably close enough to recognize the performer as something more than just a dot on the stage. Ever since our first date to a Led Zeppelin concert in 1971, Jan has always asked, "Did you get good seats?" Of course I would glow with pride in sharing how close we would be to the artists and how great our seats would be. I love the front-row view at any concert.

My daughter didn't have this in mind when she purchased the tickets for the Taylor Swift concert. When we entered the 14,000-seat arena, we trudged up and up to our seats, further and further from the stage, finally ending up in the top section in the very last row of seats; I mean, the back of my head was touching concrete. You couldn't get any further back. There I sat, the only man in the whole arena, in the worst seats in the house. The stage appeared to be over a mile away.

I looked at my daughter with *What-are-these-seats?* kind of look and she told me these were the only tickets she was able to purchase. Then came the now famous and unforgettable statement. Macie, my five-year-old granddaughter looked around and said with wonder, "Poppa, these are the best seats in the whole place. You can see everything from here!"

> The big-picture view helps you see more than what is evident, and beyond that which is right before you.

Perspective. It was all in the perspective—that big-picture view that helps you see more than what is evident, and beyond that which is right before you.

For teens today, perspective has been lost. The impact of today's actions on one's later life, the results of poor choices, and the consequences for not following rules are largely ignored because parents have lost their ability to influence their kids through giving them a *bigger picture* perspective in their parenting relationship.

Moms and Dads have moved from parenting to *peer-enting* in an attempt to create a relational environment that was perhaps not present when they were raised. That movement, coupled with a teen's perception of not needing to respect and support those in authority, has now *cut the legs off* of mom's and dad's ability to guide and influence. Teens now rely more on their peers than they do their parents, creating a *blind leading the blind* scenario that hardly fosters maturity, barely encourages responsibility, and certainly can't be a great fountain of wisdom.

Psychologist and family physician Leonard Sax states in his wonderful and insightful book, *The Collapse of Parenting*,

> The most serious consequence of the shift from a parenting-oriented culture to a peer-oriented culture is that parents no longer are able to provide that big picture to their children. (Sax, 198)

See where I'm headed?

I'm not saying parents are ineffective in their parenting. I spend two hundred nights a year on the road leading parenting conferences around the country in an attempt to help moms and dads better understand the teen world and how to counter this contrary culture working overtime to undermine their parenting roles. I do believe that parents have to be relational in their approach to their teens. They can't lead in such an authoritarian way that it pushes their child away. Instead, they need to use their God-given authority in a relational way to lead and empower their teens to be respecters of the whole family structure. And they need backup.

Parents have their hands and plates full. What their teens need is not another set of parents to complicate the already confusing roles that parents play in a culture that is overturning their efforts. What teens and parents need are people who can help bring perspective and wisdom into the family situation, to assist the parenting process by helping the kids (your grandkids) find purpose and meaning in their lives.

The people they need are you, their loving grandparents.

I bet you've stated sometime in the last few years how glad you are that you don't have to grow up in this adolescent culture. I know I would have been a mess in my junior high school years if I had access to some of the imagery and information that our grandkids are exposed to on a daily basis.

Well, your grandkids have to grow up in this culture. They have to function and survive in a world that is different from the world their parents and grandparents grew up in. That doesn't mean it is worse or bad or doomed. It just means it's different.

Different means you must approach your grandkids from a different angle, one that allows you to be invited to speak truth into their lives. Not only must you develop an understanding of what is happening in their culture, but also you have to possess the ability to see beyond what is right in front of them and offer a voice of wisdom that will guide and direct your grandkids. You can help them understand the purpose and the reasons behind what parents are asking of them. You can give them *big picture* perspective. They may have the Internet, but you have experience. They may be able to ask Siri or Alexa, but no newfangled gadget can speak truths about the meaning of life, love, and relationships. You can.

The world they live in is quite different from the one we grew up in. But it's all they know. What is totally foreign to you is absolutely common to them. Gaining an understanding of their world and their culture (without condemning or criticizing it) helps in your approach to drawing them to you as a source of wisdom.

Let me share a few of the challenges our teens face today. Not only is there a lack of respect for authority, but there is also an extreme lack of respect for one another. Media depicts politicians, pastors, police officers, teachers, administrators, businessmen and women, coaches, priests, and parents as people not worthy of respect. The current American (really, Western) culture encourages voicing disrespect of anything and anyone you don't agree with. Political correctness hampers the ability to speak freely, and the *rights of all* have so far encouraged more division than unity.

The difficulty with this culture of disrespect is that the wisdom that can be obtained from people in authority has already been tossed out before any can be transferred.

The amount of information at everyone's fingertips has overloaded our lives. Think about the number of sources of information you had when you were growing up—three main TV stations, a newspaper, and the radio. Now there are countless ways to find out everything about anything you want. The need to get information from friends and family is almost nil. Teens today are stuffed with information, yet starving for wisdom.

Think about it. Communication is at our fingertips twenty-four hours a day, seven days a week. Text messaging, apps, social media, and image messaging sites are changing the way people communicate. Dating sites now account for over fifty percent of the marriages in the U.S. Millions of pictures are sent on a daily basis, millions of videos posted on anything you can think of. Social networking sites are changing the social structure of the adolescent world, providing a false sense of connection with one another. Pornography and sexually explicit videos are readily available, changing the rules of modesty and permissible sexual behavior.

Teens today are stuffed with information, yet starving for wisdom.

Teens live in a culture where alternative lifestyles are promoted, prominent, and prevalent. Gender confusion abounds. Young men hardly know what it means to be a man, and young girls struggle to know what it is to be a woman.

There is an extreme absence of role models. Teens are becoming more and more frail. Everyone wants to be famous. Adolescents are moving more and more towards being overweight, out of shape, and suicidal. More kids are on medication than ever before.

You as a grandparent can spend time with your teen grandkids arguing any one of the above points, sharing everything that is wrong with this teen culture, but that won't build the relationship. Even though it's all true, you will accomplish nothing, except to send a clear message that you are disconnected, a *fuddy-duddy* (Does that term even still exist?), an old-timer lost in a new generation, or one who is just clueless. Yes, you can spend all your time criticizing their culture, but it will get you nowhere.

Do you have pet peeves? I have pet peeves. There are some things that just bug me and seem odd to me. I know it's a part of getting older, but there are just some elements of this culture that scream, "Danger, Will Robinson, danger!" to me. I know it's a result of this performance-driven and appearance-focused world our grandkids live in.

Here's what bugs me: It feels like people are trying to outdo and outshine each other on the Internet, seeking the false approval of social media followers instead of building real relationships with loved ones right in front of them. There are individual posts on Internet social networking sites that scream, "Will someone just look at me? Will someone just value me?"

I see a dad and daughter in a video from her wedding doing a special dance that sometimes seems like it has little to do with celebration and more to do with the need for attention. I see grandkids going to proms that have very little to do with wanting to dress up and more about showing off. I see pictures and videos of couples' wedding showers that just seem odd to me. It seems like every pregnancy now automatically comes with a *gender reveal* party. And don't get me started on the videos of people getting engaged that sometimes seem more about putting on an over-the-top show than about recording a special moment of their love for one another.

Am I revealing my age a bit? I'm sure you can list some things that bug you as well. Your pet peeves may differ from my list, but I think we all have things that bother us. Here's the best way I can handle those cultural differences and things I don't always agree with—I can keep my mouth shut. Why on earth would I do that? Why would I let my grandkids and this culture get away with all this *nonsense* when I know better? Because the Bible tells me so.

> Even fools are thought wise when they keep silent; with their mouths shut, they seem intelligent. (Proverbs 17:28, NLT)

Yep, sometimes we communicate loudest and smartest when we say nothing at all. Your role as a grandparent isn't to point out everything that's wrong with this country, this culture, and the way the world is going. Your role is to give a different perspective to your grandkids' world that, to us, appears to have gone crazy but to them is normal.

Your approach as a grandparent must be different than the approach of your grandkids' parents. If you take the same approach as their parents, their response to you will be no different than their response to their parents. They do not hear anything new. Make sense? Now I am in no way suggesting you contradict their parents. I am suggesting you act and speak in a complimentary way that backs up their parents with the same moral and spiritual truths, but delivered from different angles. You can give a bigger-picture perspective that helps grandchildren understand why their parents require things of them.

Again, it starts with first understanding the world they live in and the value of your role in their lives. You can't be a clueless outsider who just drops in from time to time with what you think is wisdom but sounds to them like a whole lot of uninformed criticism. If you don't understand, it will hamper your relationship, which prevents the transfer of biblical truths, principles, wisdom, and stories that carry on the legacy of your family.

Teens live in a world searching for someone, anyone, to listen and watch. They long for someone who understands the world and will help them understand it. They need someone who looks at life from a bigger-picture perspective and compassionately communicates the path to take to avoid mistakes and choices that can affect their lives negatively.

Perspective.

Oh yeah, back to that Taylor Swift concert. We were sitting in the back, right? My head was banging against the concrete as 13,997 little girls around me screamed at the top of their lungs throughout the whole show. Remember, these were the worst seats in the house (from my perspective). My little Macie, bless her heart, thought they were the best.

Forty-five minutes into the concert, my perspective changed too.

Much to our surprise, Taylor Swift suddenly stood singing ten feet away from us. She had come to the back (the very back) of the venue to sing right to everyone seated a million miles away from the stage. (I now see why so many adore this young lady; she loves her fans.)

Macie looked at me, eyes shining, and said, "See, Poppa, I told you these were the best seats!" She was right.

They were the best seats in the house.

It was all in the perspective.

Chapter 4

A Grandparent's
Greatest Challenge

Spend time with the wise and you will become wise,
but the friends of fools will suffer.
Proverbs 13:20 (NCV)

People have a propensity to complain about the youth of *today*. They always have. Throughout history, one can easily find moanings and groanings about these *young people* and how their attitudes and actions are destroying the very moral fiber of our country. We, meaning any of us who are older than teenagers and millennials, tend to recall our time of adolescence as a wonderful time of innocence and wonder. Nothing we did was *that bad,* certainly not as damaging and destructive as the practices of youth today. We adopt an all-is-lost attitude, thinking we are living in the worst times there have ever been.

When I think back to the time I grew up in New Orleans in the 1960s, I vividly remember the Beatles (I saw them in City Park on September 16, 1964.), the Beach Boys, the first man to walk on the moon, *The Ed Sullivan Show, Mary Poppins, The Beverly Hillbillies,* Walt Disney, Debbie Meyer swimming in the 1968 Olympics in Mexico City, Woodstock, James Bond movies, and *The Dirty Dozen,* just to name a few memories. That's what instantly comes to my mind.

When I reflect more deeply, I remember what else went on during the '60s. I come to the somewhat different conclusion that perhaps those good ol' days probably weren't as good as I thought. Vietnam, the assassination of President John F. Kennedy, the later assassination of his brother Sen. Bobby Kennedy, the assassination of Martin Luther King Jr., Louisiana's Hurricane Camille, the Bay of Pigs, the Manson murders, riots in Chicago and Detroit. Not the good ol' days, but days and years when an entire nation experienced a huge cultural shift.

Maybe it wasn't so good back then. Maybe, just maybe, it's not so bad now. Times are different. Very different. But different doesn't warrant instant judgment. Positive change rarely comes out of negative criticism. In other words, complaining doesn't fix anything.

Complaining about the youth of today is nothing new. This is what Peter the Hermit said in a sermon he preached during his lifetime. (No, Peter the Hermit was not one of Herman's Hermits.)

"The world is passing through troublous times. The young people of today think of nothing but themselves. They have no reverence for parents or old age. They are impatient of all restraint. They talk as if they knew everything, and what passes for wisdom with us is foolishness with them. As for the girls, they are forward, immodest and unladylike in speech, behavior, and dress."

French priest Peter the Hermit played a key role during the First Crusade and delivered this sermon (and his perspective on youth) more than five hundred years ago!

If you're like me, you don't want to complain all the time about the culture of teens today. Who wants to be seen as the crotchety, decrepit Grandpa instead of the fun, cool one? Instead, I want to understand today's youth culture, not frame it as an evil culture with no hope. If I see it like that, not only am I judging my grandkids and their friends, but also what hope will they have for their own futures?

I want to understand, so I can help my grandkids navigate through today's times that seem so different from the world I grew up in, yet are so similar in their challenges. One of the major challenges remains to bring timeless truth and wisdom to an ever-changing world of influence. This challenge is not the sole goal of grandparenting. First and foremost, the intent is to connect with your grandchildren during their teen years. You can be the connection that offers hope.

You can be the connection that offers hope.

You can complain about the youth of today. However, complaining always blocks the connection. Instead, I suggest you pursue ways of connecting that will move your grandchildren to bond with you so strongly that you will be able to offer them what they cannot get from any other person in the world.

I've found connection doesn't automatically happen because you are a grandparent or parent. Deep engagement isn't inherited; it's cultivated. You cultivate it every time you are intentional in reaching out to your grandchildren in ways that make them want to reach back. When you are intentional about asking for an invitation into their world instead of trying to drag them out of it and into yours, you can help your grandchildren get to the places they want to be. You can also help keep them from ending up in places they don't want to be.

This process begins with grandparents asking questions. Hopefully, it then blossoms into a relationship where the grandchild asks the questions. This exchange is a process, one I've learned from my relationships with thousands of teens

There are five necessary steps in this process of engagement and connection with your adolescent (and sometimes older) grandkids. Let's unpack them a little here.

Show Interest

During the first years of our grandkids' lives, I think we get involved for our own selfish reasons. We love their cuteness, enjoy watching them grow, feel ecstatic when they give us a name (no matter how corny or funny those names may be. I know one set of grandparents whose grandson thought *Grandma* and *Grandpa* sounded like *Gravy* and *Meatball*. The names stuck.) Grandbabies make us feel good, look good, and put a smile on our face. I don't think there's anything wrong with our intentions at this point. Pride in your progeny (once removed) is pretty normal.

Then those cute little grandkids turn twelve, and it all begins to change. That is exactly when we grandparents better change right with them. Adolescence is a critical point that could determine your level of involvement in the rest of their lives. During this critical time, you have to shift the focus of your relationship from your interests to theirs.

If your grandchild feels for a moment that your purpose and intent in their life is just to transfer all the wisdom you've gained in life, you will bore them to tears. You will quickly find yourself irrelevant in their lives. It will be apparent to them that you are in this thing to fulfill your own agenda, not because you care about them. They will see it as nothing more than another program that is more about you than them. They can smell that a mile away. You may think adolescents and teens have no common sense, but they can be incredibly savvy. And they can quickly spot a fake. Remember, grandparenting is not about you. It's about your grandkids.

> Grandparenting is not about you. It's about your grandkids.

Paul writes about this when he says to the Philippians,

> Do nothing out of selfish ambition or vain conceit. Rather, in humility value others above yourselves, not looking to your own interests but each of you to the interests of the others. (Philippians 2:3-4)

The second part of this *shifting* is changing the focus of your interest. One of the hardest challenges of grandparenting is sharing the wisdom you have gathered through life in a way that applies to *their* world and *their* culture, not the world you grew up in and learned from.

I know teens show an interest in me because I have an interest in them. They are longing for someone to listen to their hearts and their stories. They want to be loved and cared for beyond the five love languages. They want to do things together. They want to eat where they want to eat, go where they want to go, and have someone help them fulfill their dreams. Showing interest in your grandkids isn't something you do; it must become who you are.

Adapt to Their World

Okay, so you live in a world of immodest girls who are unladylike in their behavior, foolish boys who think only of themselves, a world where kids have a great sense of entitlement. They are impatient, know everything, and hardly respect their elders. That is exactly how Peter the Hermit saw it way back around A.D. 1080. (By the way, the lead singer of Herman's Hermits *was* a guy named Peter—Peter Noonan.) That is the world of kids today, and in every age, it seems. But it's the world your grandkids have to live in.

Those are the cards you've been dealt. They're more than just cards; they're the grandkids you love. If you want to be an influence and make an impact on their lives, then you will have to adapt your message so it includes an understanding of the world they live in.

When I say adapt, I'm not telling you to scrap your standards or beliefs and discard what you hold to be true and valuable. I am telling you that your message has to apply to their world. You can't be a stick (in the mud), but pliable and adjustable to wrap around the issues they are facing. Usually, people who criticize the cards they've been dealt can't adapt. That gives them very little ability to speak into the lives of their teen grandchildren.

You'll be like the major department stores and companies we see going belly up. They couldn't adapt to the changing times and keep up with the transformation and conversion of a culture that has made some pretty extreme shifts in the last few years. So they closed up shop. Don't close the doors on the teens you love.

If your message is relevant, don't change your content. Do change the way you approach it and say it so the intended recipients of the message can embrace the message, engage with applicability, and value the effectiveness of the wisdom shared.

As I travel across North America, I see a great decline in church attendance by those about to graduate from high school and those in their late teens. In other words, there are about a million kids in the seventh-grade youth program and about four who remain in the church by their senior year. Okay, I may be exaggerating and joking a little here, but there is a major drop. This age group tends to take a hiatus from church, and I think they do so for a couple of adaptability reasons.

The first reason is that many teens believe the church isn't that important. The busyness of their schedules coupled with other interests crowds out time for church and church-related activities. The second reason is that youth leaders have been slow to adapt the gospel message to an age group that has gone through major, radical upheavals in its socialization process. I'm not faulting youth guys (or gals). The immense and rapid changes within the youth culture caught them off guard. But these two reasons speak volumes to the need for the adaptability of the message to a new, tech-savvy but relationship-poor generation that often overwhelmed by life as they know it.

Adaptability is more than the pastor wearing an untucked shirt and ripped or even skinny jeans. It's more than current and contemporary worship songs with lights down low and a few candles burning through the fog machine. It is understanding the needs and speaking directly to the issues that teens are facing, then giving directives that speak directly to those problems and matters in a way that doesn't alienate teens.

Build Relationship

A real relationship takes the investment of time, effort, and resources as mentioned earlier in this book. The key word is *investment*. The focus of that investment has to be the benefit of the grandchild, motivated out of love for that child.

Paul wrote to the Thessalonians and said,

"We loved you so much that we shared with you not only God's Good News but our own lives, too." (1 Thessalonians 2:8)

Teens are looking for genuineness, authenticity, and relationships that offer something more than only correction when they mess up. They desire someone who is frank, honest and isn't afraid to speak the truth in love because they know the motivation comes from a deep empathy for their plight.

> A teen listens to authority because of relationship.

If you have a discipline problem, you have a relationship problem. If you have a respect problem, you have a relationship problem. If you have an obedience problem, you have a relationship problem. In a relationship, you will see the problems, and in a relationship, you will discover a teen's motivation for change. A teen does not change because of an authoritarian approach. A teen listens to authority because of relationship.

Your relationship with your grandchildren could be the only voice of wisdom they listen to, in a time of their lives when they aren't listening to God or any other member of their family. You could be the only attachment they have to the family when they feel distant from siblings and parents who are disappointed and upset with their choices.

The need to have fun together is paramount. How much you laugh together is a good measurement of your relationship. The amount of communication between you and your grandchildren will be an indicator of how healthy your relationship is.

So learn every way possible to communicate as a grandparent, not a parent. Your role is not to be a second set of parents, but one who encourages and communicates hope and perspective. As you move into antiquity, be sure to try to keep up with technology so you maintain and entertain new forms of communication. If you don't know how to do this, ask the kids. They'll be happy to teach you, and it will give you an opportunity to learn something new together.

Create Connection

The connection I'm talking about is the next step in the relationship with your grandchild. This connection is more than you making things happen. It's when communication, effort, and desire to spend time together become a two-way street. This is what you want to happen with your teenage grandchildren. It is more important than the message you have to share. It has to be cultivated…and watered…and fertilized…and allowed to grow.

Let me give you an example. My granddaughter Maile and I love country music. She knows the lyrics to every current country song. How she does it, I'll never know. Because of her love for this genre of music, I joined the Country Music Association so we could attend the Country Music Awards every year. I purchase the tickets, book the flight, and we go. We laugh, take pictures, laugh more, cheer on the artists, and leave Nashville with memories that will last her a lifetime. I purchase shirts and programs for her and provide opportunities for her to meet as many artists as I can. It's all for one purpose—to keep the connection we've found and hopefully nurture it until my dying day.

We text each other with news about upcoming concerts and up-and-coming artists. We look together for the next opportunity to spend time at these events. The result? A special connection that ties our hearts together. It is a tie that binds when other things in her life aren't quite as she or her parents hope they will be. The connection has been a lifeline for Maile and me.

So here are some things I've learned about connection with grandkids:

- Connection is more than just a relationship (Why anyone can have that!); it's a conduit for providing hope and direction.
- Connection is not just making sure you have a great Christmas pic of all your family to send out to friends.
- Connection is not measured by the number of pictures of your grandchild you post on your social networking sites.

- Connection is not just appearing to have a relationship; connection is having the relationship that is measured by two-way efforts to remain engaged with one another.
- Connection is not an opportunity for correction.
- Connection is a mutual love for one another established because a grandparent determines to pour life and love into a child who longs to be connected with family.

Invite Questions

When I initially show interest in any teen, including my grandkids, I do it by asking questions about his or her life, thoughts, and heart. It's not the interrogating type of questioning that puts them on the spot or makes them feel like I'm looking for problems, but the type of questions that convey value.

The questions I ask also give them an example of what's it like to show interest in others, to consider others more important than oneself.

My hope is they'll begin to ask me questions because they see me as a grandparent full of wisdom (not correction), one who genuinely is focused on bettering their lives, one who is willing to put his money where his mouth is and share time, effort, and resources to further the relationship.

This is what I want to happen: I want them to start asking me questions. You'll know you have a connection when your grandkids start asking in some shape or form any of the following questions:

- Can you keep a secret?
- Can I tell you something?
- Hey, want to get together for dinner?
- Grandpa, did you ever smoke pot or get drunk?
- Grandma, did you and Grandpa ever have sex before you got married?
- Grandpa, what if I marry the wrong person?
- Grandma, did you ever fall away from Jesus...I mean, just not get it sometimes?

- Hey, what's the one life lesson you've found to be the most important?

As a grandparent, this is what you've been waiting for. It's their invitation to you to speak the truth (however painful that may be) into their lives. They're asking because they want answers. Their questions will let you know there is a connection, and they want wisdom.

Over time, you'll find that talking about the hard stuff and sharing the reality of the lessons you've learned will convey those rare qualities of good relationships called genuineness and authenticity—two items in high demand in today's teen culture.

They are learning. You can be a safe place, a sounding board as they learn how to function in their culture in a healthy way. They're just doing it differently than you did. I assure you they will learn what they need to learn to survive in their world. Hopefully, they'll do it with a foundation of wisdom that you speak into their lives, so their learning isn't quite as painful as your acquisition of wisdom was. It's one of the greatest challenges of grandparents, but so well worth the effort.

> Grandparenting is more about who you *are* in the presence of your grandkids.

Quit complaining about your grandkids. Begin the trek to building a relationship that connects you to the very heart of your grandchildren. Remember, it's not about what you *do*, and it's not necessarily about what you *say*. It's more about who you *are* in the presence of your grandkids.

PART II — YOUR PRESENCE

Chapter 5

Why Gray Hair Works to Your Benefit

The glory of young men is their strength,
but the splendor of old men is their gray hair.
Proverbs 20:29 (ESV)

What do your grandkids call you?

Soon-to-be grandparents wrangle over what they want to be called. I tell them it doesn't matter what the kids call you. You'll love whatever name they attach to you.

I've heard some crazy ones just to prove my point. Who would have thought that some grandparents would be called any of these following names and like it?

Busoma, BooBoo, Oompa, Suggy, Bop-Bop, Botchie, Amma, GaGa, Bearbsie and Poppa Bear, Bla-Bla (now, that's an interesting one), Birdie, Big Grandpa, Bomp, and of course, Bobaloo.

Call grandparents whatever you want, make fun of all the various nicknames, but when that child calls you by that special name, there's just something that makes a grandparent feel wanted and needed.

My grandkids call me *Poppa* in front of me. I'm sure they say other things behind my back. But *Poppa* pretty much gets my full attention.

Once I was in Moscow, Russia, a young girl ran up to me and said, "Poppa!" Evidently, that's a common word for fathers in Russia, and she immediately had my attention. She then said, "Take me!" She said only three words, but because she said "Poppa," she had my immediate attention. I felt I should do whatever she said. I even called Jan and told her we should adopt her. There's something special that happens when you hear the name you were given by a grandchild.

Whatever your grandchildren call you, I'm sure it's a term of endearment that means a lot to you. I mean, who else could call you Birdie and Bop-Bop, introduce you to their friends like that, and get away with it? Ha! Why even my oldest granddaughter's friends call me *Poppa*. There's something about that position in their lives I don't want to lose.

I must say I spoil my grandkids. I give them just about anything they want. It's what grandparents are supposed to do. When they want to go somewhere, want something special, and *need* something, I'm pretty much a sucker for helping any way I can.

As they get older, I want to keep that same position in their lives. I want to connect when going somewhere, wanting something, and needing more can't be satisfied by the expenditure of cash but by the dispelling and disbursement of wisdom and counsel.

Please hear once again that my intent isn't to circumvent or go around the parents as if to somehow hold a higher position in a child's life. That's not the intent at all. There's something very wrong about the intentions of grandparents who feel they are better or want to replace the position parents have in the lives of their children.

My intent is to be a helpmate to my kids and to support and encourage their desires for their kids. A voice from outside the home (a grandparent's voice) can affirm and support, as well as uphold rules, expectations, and the desires of the parents in the lives of grandkids. I want to help my kids and grandkids by giving a different perspective that still ends up at the same place. It just approaches that place from a different path. You can too.

If the position you developed in the earlier years can be further developed during the adolescent years, then that position can offer wisdom in a way that helps explain and give reasons for the rules and restrictions parents often have to place on kids.

Maybe it's the gray hair that attracts kids to me. Or maybe it's the mustache I wear from the 1880's that reassures them they're talking to an old guy who might just have some answers or give some understanding to anything confusing. I want to think I've earned every one of my gray hairs. I'm proud of them even though when they began showing up on my head I plucked them out as if embarrassed to be getting older.

Proverbs 16:31 (NRSV) affirms my love of my gray hair: "Gray hair is a crown of glory; it is gained in a righteous life."

Darn right, it is. And I'm going to use it any way I can to benefit those around me.

When I was a Young Life leader, I thought I would lose my effectiveness by age twenty-five. I thought maybe I would be too old by that age. Then as a youth minister, I thought my gig would be up at thirty when I crossed over the hill. When kids came to live with Jan and me at Heartlight, I began to think, "Okay, by forty, kids will stop listening to me." In my forties, I thought the half-century mark would close down the stream of teens coming to me to talk. Then I turned fifty, and one day as I was plucking out gray hairs, it occurred to me I was no longer a *young thang* kids wanted to talk to. I was a guy who was showing his age and teens actually wanted more.

Now that I'm sixty, I've come to realize that age and a little gray hair (actually, a lot of it) is a magnet to teens that want wisdom. Now I'm working hard to keep all this gray stuff I have. I've put away the tweezers and feel pretty comfortable with this aging process. It affords me a different spot in the lives of my grandkids they can get from no one else.

They're searching for wisdom. What they are getting from their peers, television, and the Internet is an overwhelming flow of information that doesn't always have substance. It's easy to find information, but not context or truth. Siri, Alexa, or anyone who has a smart phone can tell you what time it is or help you order a pizza. They can't help you ponder the real meaning of life or how a lifelong relationship really works. I want to give them what they can't find anywhere else by maintaining a special connection with them that is irreplaceable and offers wisdom—wisdom that takes into account the faults, struggles, makeup, genetics, history, tradition, and difficulties within this thing called *family*. Wisdom shared with perspective.

Wisdom is so much more than a collection of astute and sensible words shared at the right time. Teens have heard enough words through the bombardment of information. They desire for the "word to become flesh" (See John 1:14.) and to see the application of all they have been taught through the years. It's basically their plea of, "Don't tell me. Show me."

Granddad, or whatever name you go by, don't worry you're not saying the right thing. Many men feel inadequate like they lack wise words to share at the right time. That's okay. Your teen grandkids aren't buying the words they hear any more; they want to see those words in action.

Grandmas, or if your grandkids call you Amma or Bop-Bop (great names, eh?), it's not about your words once they reach the teen years. Quit talking so much and start showing them how your words line up with your actions. Talk less. Show more.

Here are the ways teens pick up wisdom:

Observation

They're watching you. In their quietness and cognitive processing, your grandkids are seeing whether your actions support the words you say. It's how they determine if the truth they hear is truthful enough to be fleshed out in real life.

They watch you in your everyday interactions with other drivers, waitresses, flight attendants, fellow workers, employees, landscapers, and those you do business with. They witness how you talk to your spouse, how you treat the dog, how you handle conflict, how much you laugh, how much you cry, and how much you hurt. They look at what you look at, what you read, how you care for folks who have less than you, how you treat other kids, and how you act toward those who hurt you and those who love you.

They are processing traits like forgiveness, grace, love, empathy, sympathy, encouragement, boldness, and integrity by comparing what they see vs. what they've been taught for so many years.

> In order to see and observe, it's imperative that time is spent together.

In order to see and observe, it's imperative that time is spent together. One can't see what isn't there. Presence (not presents) is key to having an impact on the life of your grandkids and maintaining that relationship through their teen years.

Reflection

When your grandkids leave your presence, what do they think about? Do you leave them thinking about anything?

Reflection happens when a grandchild considers what you said or what they saw in your actions. Sometimes you may leave them with a question rather than always giving them the answers. Or it may be a statement given, not to show what a gray-headed stud you are, but to provoke their thinking.

Look, I believe most of your grandkids have grown up in a world where the seeds of truth have been scattered throughout their life. When they reach their teen years, we need to scale back on planting and spend more time cultivating. Cultivation includes turning the soil, adding fertilizer, watering, providing light, and sometimes pulling weeds. All these actions have a way of disrupting (in a good way) the landscape of your grandchild's heart to get them to internalize what they have been taught. Cultivation can move them out of dormancy into productivity.

Encouraging reflection is a way of engaging your grandchildren to take responsibility for their thinking and process life in a way that moves them on to emotional and spiritual maturity.

Try this. The next time you see one of your grandkids, find a quiet time to share with them. Tell them, "There's nothing you can do to make me love you more, and there's nothing you can do to make me love you less." It's a powerful statement that lets them know of your undying love for them, and it also gets them to think about your relationship. Teens know people love them when they're doing well; I'm not sure they believe that to be true when they're not.

Shift the way you engage with your grandkids, and you'll shift their desire from wanting just dollars from you to wanting more, something they can't get anywhere else.

Experience

I used to think if I didn't pray at the table before a meal or have a devotion at some opportune time or say something spiritual at the right moment, my kids or grandkids would never get to see the deep love I have for God or experience the joy I have because of a relationship with Him. I don't think that anymore.

I now believe the experiences we share together have an amazing way of communicating not only what I do, but also who I am. Let me repeat this again. The emotions of a lifetime are often found in the all-but-forgotten experiences of adolescence. It's an important statement.

I do believe as we hide God's Word in our heart, memorize His truth, and internalize His love for us, the expression of Him comes out at the most unexpected times. It sometimes comes out in the form of laughter. Or is articulated in a discussion that doesn't fall back on *Christianese* but is principled on truth. It can be communicated through conversations that toss in golden nuggets of truth and wisdom that can only come from God himself. Or it can be uttered in the most amazing and surprising locations and situations where we least expect it.

> Your actions do speak louder than your words.

At this point, your actions do speak louder than your words. As you experience travel, meals, special occasions, vacations, funerals, weddings, and plenty of normal interactions, God will allow His Word to become flesh through you.

Spend more time lining up experiences than giving things that are one day going to rot, get destroyed, or become outdated. Buy a boat or a WaveRunner. Get that house at the lake. Buy a new grill for your patio and grill the greatest meals of all time. Go on a hunting trip. Take a trip to New York with your granddaughters. Go to concerts. Attend the Country Music Awards. Take a trip to the Grand Canyon. Go skiing (water or snow). Take a trip to the beach. Plan things that include your grandkids.

I owned a Harley and realized it was something my grandkids couldn't do with me. I see grandparents purchasing RV's and leaving their family behind to travel the country. I see other grandparents retiring and moving to where they can do what they've always wanted to do. They take up hobbies that don't include the grandkids. There's nothing wrong with any of these, but I would encourage you to plan and create experiences often with your

> Love means sometimes giving up your right to your own fun in order to show love by having fun with your teen grandchildren.

grandchildren. They should know their grandparents aren't just people who have fun but are people who are fun to be with because of the shared experiences grandparents and grandchildren enjoy together.

Wisdom can be found in the lives of grandparents who have a wealth of insight and understanding, but it can only be imparted if those grandparents create an environment for their grandkids to discover it in them. Love means sometimes giving up your right to your own fun in order to show love by having fun with your teen grandchildren. I promise it's worth every bit of the sacrifice to leave a legacy of love.

Chapter 6

Changing Gears When You're Almost Out of Gas

From everyone who has been given much, much will be
demanded; and from the one who has been entrusted
with much, much more will be asked.
Luke 12:48

It's time to change gears. Shift those gears before you run out of gas.

Even if your gears are rusty, you can't get stuck in neutral, drive, or reverse and be a truly successful grandparent. You have to shift gears at the right times to meet the changing needs of your grandkids and their parents. In the teen years, you even have to get out of the car and let your grandkids take a turn at the wheel. I have more to say about that later in this chapter.

For now, remember what you read earlier about how grandparents need to shift their style of grandparenting and *change gears* to accommodate the needs of their children's children? The time is now, as they become teens and young adults. If grandparents don't, then the only stories shared as people remember your legacy will be those that occurred when your grandchildren were little.

If you don't switch your grandparenting style from the way you parented or were parented, you'll be out of touch, as antiquated as your grandmother's sewing machine. You may be accused of never letting those special kids grow into the people God destined them to be. Nor will you get to have any of the deep discussions that will sprout from all the hard-earned wisdom you attained.

The first twelve years of your grandkids' lives are a time of teaching. A time where parents pour into their kids and allow them to be involved in everything the Christian world has to offer. It's a time of planting seeds and imparting the need to follow the biblical principles that parents hold dear to their heart.

It's the parents' responsibility to plant these seeds of faith, not the grandparents (unless the grandparents are raising the grandkids). I say this because I have seen more times than I would ever have imagined how grandparents don't feel like the parents are instilling enough of a Christian lifestyle into the hearts of the grandkids, so the grandparents have to intervene to make up the difference between so-so and great teaching.

Well intended but grossly misunderstood, the messages grandparents many times send to their grandkids through texts, specialty cards, and other communiqués are interpreted as a judgment rather than encouragement. Let me say again that the grandparents' role during the teen years is to cultivate the soil to hold the seeds planted through the parents' efforts in a grandchild's earlier years. When grandparents try to teach when what is needed is training, everyone gets frustrated.

Let me be clear here. You have a role in the lives of your grandkids. If you want to fulfill that role to the fullest during their teen years, be the one who helps in the training process. Take what has been taught and help them apply truth to their lives. Be as effective as you can in fulfilling the role that is greatly lacking and significantly needed in their lives. There's no one else who can do this as well as you because of the position God has placed you in.

Stated as simply as I can, when your grandchildren enter their teen years, you must switch your model of influence from teaching to training. To explain what I mean, let me break it down into a list of what you must move from and move to.

Move from Allowing Immaturity to Encouraging Maturity

Twelve-year-olds are expected to be immature because they are. As they turn thirteen, it's important that everyone involved in the life of the child begins the push to maturity. Grandparents are no exception. A grandparent's home is not to be a place where a young thirteen- to fourteen-year-old can retreat and escape the growing-up process. That would be in direct conflict with the desires of the parents.

When your grandchildren enter their teen years, you must switch your model of influence from teaching to training.

No one wants to have a twenty-five-year-old lounge lizard hanging out on the sofa playing video games with no job, no drive, and no direction in life. Hopefully, you didn't let your kids do that. Don't allow your grandkids to think they can do that with you. Once they enter the teen years, it's time to start growing up.

Encouraging maturity includes, but is not limited to, all the items I've listed below. The real challenge in this changing of the gears is in the mindset of the parents and grandparents. Instead of looking at your child (or grandchild) as this neat little kid and enjoying every part of him or her, the focus should be on a time of preparation for what you want to see in the future.

It is shifting gears from a teaching model to a training model. Teaching is the gear all should be engaged in the first twelve years. Training is the next gear. Might I remind you that this is not automatic? It will not happen on its own or by itself. It's a determined conviction on the part of parents and grandparents to push, allow, and focus on helping children take what they have been taught and put it into play in their life. Then they can mature and develop out of a self-centered, entitled mindset where they wake up in the morning and ask, "What's everyone going to do for me today?"

Move from Dependence on You to Developing Independence

Children are dependent on their parents and grandparents for everything. If the goal is to help your grandchildren develop a healthy independence by the time they reach the age of eighteen, then the training has to happen now as they leave childhood behind and enter adolescence and teens. Teaching gives them the tools; training allows them to use them.

Chances are, everyone has been doing pretty much everything for your grandchild up to this point. Someone has made all their decisions, taken responsibilities for every area of their life, had total control of behavior, given them all the answers, and lectured until they're blue in the face. If you don't switch gears, you'll end up with that twenty-five-year-old I mentioned earlier.

Here are some examples that might help you understand this a little better. If a child is taught about school, the need to do homework, and the importance of good grades, then at some point the child must be allowed to determine when to study, expected to hand in their own work, and even take the risk of failing. If and when they experience failure, they begin to learn that not everyone else is going to do the work for them. They must do it.

It's funny to have all the parents and grandparents at the science fair laugh about how much work they put into their fourth graders' science projects. Parents and grandparents come up with a good idea, do all the work, and pretty much oversee the whole project. It really is kind of funny. But it's not that funny when the kids hit ninth grade. Matter of fact, it would be rather sad. The problem is not the child. It's the parents and grandparents encouraging immaturity rather than taking the opportunity to encourage maturity.

Here is another example. From the ages of one to twelve years, you and your grandchildren's parents have told and taught the grandchildren what to do in a particular situation. When you begin to switch to the training model, you move from telling them what they must do to asking, "What do you think you ought to do?"

Posing the question to the children means they'll have to dig through their memory banks and pull out the file of what they were taught to do in that kind of situation. This is where parents and grandparents allow the child to begin the critical thinking process. They haven't had to think before because everyone did it for them. It is imperative that it becomes their turn to figure it out long before life forces them to do it on their own.

This training model means that instead of you (as parent or grandparent) taking the ball and running with it, you toss it to them and let them run. Will they stumble? Sure they will. Just like you did the first time you were given a chance to run with the ball. If they do stumble, they'll get back up because you shifted gears from being a teacher and moved into the role of trainer. As the trainer on the sidelines, you encourage them to brush off their knees and keep going. Then you cheer them on.

Move from Your Decisions to Helping Them Learn to Make Their Decisions

Decision-making is important. If you want your grandchild to be able to make big and important decisions later in life, you've got to give them the opportunity to flex their decision-making muscle. The more they work out now, the better shape they'll be in when they are truly out on their own. Is it easier, more time saving, and far more convenient to keep making the decisions ourselves? Absolutely. Does it stunt the growth of our grandkids' maturity? Absolutely.

Let them decide when they need to study for school. Now, if you have a child who can't stop playing video games or gets consumed with chatting or texting friends, then, sure, you've got to intervene. Where there are no internal boundaries, grandparents (and parents) have to establish external boundaries.

By thirteen years of age, it would greatly help a child to be able to decide what they are going to wear to school. At some point, they need to determine whether they're going to brush their teeth, wear sunscreen at the beach (kind of a learn or burn), or purchase new clothes (even with your money).

It's hard to break them from being dependent on you to make their own decisions because it's easier for them to let you do it as well. Plus, if they make a mistake in their decisions, they might just blame the outcome on you because you didn't do what you were supposed to do. You and I know transferring the responsibility to make good decisions is a process. It will take time, but is well worth the effort as your grandchildren progress through adolescence.

Let them begin to decide where to eat dinner. What TV programs to watch. What time to go to bed. What music to listen to. Whether or not they play sports. At some point, which church they go to or whether they go at all. Who they're going to date.

Whether they need a job. How they spend their Saturdays. Who their friends are.

Remember that the goal here is allowing them to flex those decision-making muscles while you're still around to ultimately help lift the weight off their chest if it falls. Then there is still time to have those deeper discussions about what happened when they made a mistake or a not-so-good choice and what they could do better next time.

I'm not encouraging you as a grandparent to allow every decision to be made by your grandchild. There have got to be some home rules in place, so a grandchild knows that some decisions have already been made for them. Yes, you do want your home to be a place of rest for your grandkids, but you don't want it to be a place that is out of control where they get to do anything and everything they want. Rules without relationship may cause rebellion. Relationships without rules cause chaos.

Move from You Doing It to Them Doing It

Quit doing everything for them. Revolving our lives around our kids and grandkids is easy. But if entitlement and selfishness run rampant in a culture that is *all about me,* then you are the ones to break that cycle. If you don't, then you will have spoiled brats on your hands who enter their twenties about to head into disaster. Their health may take a beating, lives may derail, or marriages may fail.

In an effort to help kids understand I'm not their servant, maid, tutor, slave, or employee, I tell them, "I owe you nothing, but I want to give you everything. Still, I owe you nothing." It changes their perspective when I do things for them or help them in any way. I want them to be responsible for their own lives and break the habit of selfishness supported by their *culture of me.*

Now if I do anything for them or give them anything, it's an act of grace and not a fulfillment of obligation or entitlement. That is an important concept for them to embrace. It's an idea that will change their future relationships.

> Quit doing everything for your grandchildren.

In the teen years, it's time for them to start doing their own laundry. Let them pack for their own vacation. Let them choose their own hairstyle. Let them purchase their own clothes, no matter how awful they look. Let them put their own gas in the car. Let them learn how to use an alarm clock now, so you don't have eighteen-year-olds in college who can't get out of bed. Let them be responsible for their own academics, and let them take their own clothes to the cleaners.

Quit doing everything for them.

Move from Your Control to Their Control

The only way a child will learn to take control of his life and develop the need for self-control is by a parent and grandparent letting go. Give teens control. In the early years, you have total control of your grandchild. You make all the decisions, do everything for them, and have full responsibility for their lives. Changing gears can be hard at age thirteen when you begin to realize that you don't have that much control over them anymore anyway. So hand some of it over before it gets wrestled away from you. It's much more effective and relationship-building that way.

Attempts to take control from them may prevent them from learning self-control. You want them to be in control. Don't you? I do! I want my grandchildren to have control when they get pulled over by a policeman for speeding. I want them to have control with a girlfriend or boyfriend. I want them to learn restraint with their words when they're provoked. I want them to embrace the concept of keeping their mouths shut when it would be easier to fire off comments that will only cause more damage.

I tell the kids who live with us that I really don't care whether they pass or flunk their classes at our school. Isn't that a great thing to say to students, coming from a founder of a boarding school? Truth be told, I do care. But I don't accept responsibility for their academics. I tell them they have control and can make the decision to complete high school whenever they want. It is my way of giving up control and giving it to them.

Move from Giving Answers to Asking Questions

As grandparents, we always have a comment, an answer, or the right way of doing things. Shoot, you know we do. It's because we're good, we know what's right, and if everyone would just do it our way, we'd all be better off. I chuckle as I write this because there is some truth in my comments. You and I can be the greatest deterrents to our grandchildren's search for answers because we know all the answers. Ha!

I encourage you to do this. Quit being the answer man or answer woman. Begin to let your grandkids do some searching on their own. If they don't learn it now, they'll only have to learn it when they're apart from us.

You're used to giving answers in their early years. That's what teaching is all about. Now that the gears are shifting in our grandparenting, you must stop giving the answers and start asking more questions to help your grandkids learn to process on their own.

Your conversations should contain phrases like the following:

- What do you think we should do in this situation?
- What would you do if you were in that position?

- What do you think would be the best alternative to resolve this issue?
- Did you think that was fair?
- Would you have done the same thing?
- What do you think is the greatest struggle teens face today?
- What do you think about the legalization of marijuana?
- Do you think politics are as messy as they seem?

When your grandchildren answer, hold your tongue and don't correct. Keep yourself from telling them where they are wrong. Refrain from sharing your opinion. Simply let the discussion happen. If they ask you what you think, even then you should not always answer. Many times your answer will stop the conversation (because you probably just shared the best answer. What else can your grandchild add at that point?). If you want them to come to the right answer themselves, let them figure it out. Don't give it to them.

Please beware of this: no manipulation. Don't ask questions so that you can listen to what they have to say and gain a platform to share your opinion. This is what I call *selfish questioning* because it's not really about your grandchild. It's more about your need to talk.

Always ask questions. Quit giving the answers.

Move from Punishment to Their Understanding of the Value in Discipline

Punishment used to be easy to dole out when your grandchildren were little—violate the home policy, get into trouble. It was all about following your rules, doing what you said, without question. Punishment steered them away from wrong choices. It gave them understanding that good choices bring pleasure and foolish choices bring pain. Punishment kept foolish choices from happening (or at least nipped them in the bud).

Now you're moving away from punishment into a world of discipline, hopefully with the end goal of self-discipline. Discipline now helps a child get where they want to go, and keeps them from ending up in a place they don't want to be. It's not about the infliction of pain.

71

It emphasizes making good decisions. Discipline lets adolescents and teens know you're working with them in their choices to help, not to force them to do or not do things.

When teens know you're working with them and want to help get them to a better place in life, they'll welcome the limits, restrictions, and boundaries set around them. When they believe you're just out to punish them, they push back hard against your limits.

Move from Your Responsibility to Encouraging Their Responsibility

Parents and grandparents naturally make all decisions for infants and very young children. They are totally dependent on adults for everything in life. As children grow, parents and grandparents still make the vast majority of decisions in a child's life. If that pattern continues into the teen years, it fosters trouble for teens and the adults who love them. As kids enter their teen years, the greatest gift a parent or grandparent can give is to engage the children in the process of accepting making choices so they can learn to accept responsibility for their own lives. This, in turn, will produce emotional, spiritual, and relational maturity.

Maturity is a by-product of responsibility. If anyone in the family prevents a child's acceptance of responsibility for his own life, then they are doing too much for that child, i.e. making too many decisions, keeping the control, and refusing to trust the child.

Remember the verse from the beginning of this chapter? Let's re-read it. Luke 12:48 states something I believe is key to the training process.

> From everyone who has been given much, much will be demanded; and from the one who has been entrusted with much, much more will be asked.

What I'm proposing in this training model is the transfer of quite a bit to your grandkids. While this means they'll experience more freedom in their pursuit of independence, it also means more will be required from your grandchildren as well.

Move from Lecturing to Having Discussions

This one is easy. Move from all those lectures that you realize are producing nothing and begin to have discussions full of opinions, questions, differing thoughts, and controversial stances. Remember, your discussions are no longer going to be little quips of words where all the world's problems are solved in a few minutes. Most discussions are composed of many conversations over a period of time. Often, you will not be able to solve any of the world's problems. And even if you think you can, it's wise to keep the solution to yourself and see if your grandchildren can come to the same conclusion by themselves.

Remember, you want to keep the conversation going. Your goal is to be a place of wisdom your grandchild can visit over and over again.

Move from Telling to a Model of Sharing

Along the same vein of having discussions, movement from the teaching to the training model means a shift in the way you distribute what you have to say. It can no longer be, "This is the way it is. Period." It's got to be more of a, "This is what I think." Or, "This is what I believe."

Many times I ask teens if they want a response from me. I ask, "Do you want an answer or my opinion?" Sometimes, they say "neither." I leave it at that. Successful grandparents with strong connections and relationships are okay leaving it right there. They know it creates a safe place for teens to hash out what they're trying to work out. It also leaves the door open for them to come back and ask for that advice or opinion later if they can't figure it out.

Move from Talking to Listening

Here's another tough one. The times when you used to just talk to your grandkids need to be replaced with spending more time listening once they enter their teen years. Many times, kids tell me that the ol' grandfolks just like to hear themselves talk and never listen to what the teen wants to say.

Listen well to hear the heartbeat of your grandchild.

As one grandparent to another, you've had your time to talk. Now it is your time to listen. Listen well to hear the heartbeat of your grandchild.

How would you rather be known? As one who talked all the time or one who was a great listener? Wise grandparents desire the latter.

Listen.

Move the Emphasis from What You Do to Who You Are

Making the transition from what you do for your kids and grandkids to who you are at your core is an evolution and conversion individual to each grandparent. When you are doing, it has more to do with behavior. When you shift to showing who you are, you reveal your character. Many times parents are more concerned about the everyday, surface behavior they see and experience rather than working on the heart and building their grandchildren's character. Grandparents can hone in on those occasional momentary glimpses of greatness and help their grandkids see it in themselves too.

A grandparent's voice of wisdom gives grandchildren the perspective that life is more than just a series of behaviors to be praised or corrected. Grandparents help grandchildren understand that their greatness may feel locked inside for now but will soon be revealed in who they become. It's a message of hope and promise that can only come from a grandparent who is more concerned about where they are headed than where they have been.

As a final word about gear shifting from teaching to training, let me share this: If parents make this transition and grandparents don't, then Grandpa and Grandma will be ignored and placed on the shelf. Along with their shelving will be all the great wisdom and insight they possess. Kids want to grow up. They want to take responsibility for their lives. They want to make decisions. They want to be mature. They want to be in control. They will always side with those who help them move toward independence and resist those who impede their progress.

Make sure they side with you. Move over to the passenger side and hand over the keys of decision-making before you run out of gas. It may be a wild ride at first, but the journey is thrilling and the destination well worth the price!

Chapter 7

Maintaining Your Relationship in a Not-So-Relational Culture

Therefore let us not pass judgment on one another any
longer, but rather decide never to put a stumbling
block or hindrance in the way of a brother.
Romans 14:13 (ESV)

I really feel that grandkids are a reward for not killing your own kids. I'm joking. I'm joking. (Okay, not really.)

I love my grandkids. Matter of fact, I think I love them more than my own kids.

My daughter recently looked at me and said, "Dad, it's almost as if you like them more than us." I replied with a smirk on my face and a little bit of truth in my tone, "Is it that evident?"

There is something very, very special about a relationship with your grandchildren. There is no other relationship quite like it. When I am a great-grandparent, and my daughter is a grandparent, I am sure she will understand.

As I watch my grandkids grow and change, the type of relationship I have with them changes too. It's not just making the changes of moving from a teaching model to a training model. It also includes changing some attitudes I've carried for quite a few years. The reason for the change? So I can maintain the relationship that began the day these grandkids were born.

Remember that tingle in your heart the first time you held them? Recall the joy? If you are like me, there was a little voice that bounced around in your head, saying, *God has truly blessed me with something special.* My grandkids show me a place in my heart I never knew existed.

Well, when that ball of specialness reaches those adolescent years, they need you just as much, but you may feel like they're trying to push you away. Their busy schedule seems geared to push you out.

Your grandkids need relationships—good, lasting, committed relationships that don't stop when they don't respond. They need strong grandparent ties that weather the every-other-week stormy times of adolescence. They especially need a deep relationship with their grandparents because they're not getting those relational needs filled by their peers—at least not in wise, healthy ways. Our grandkids and their friends spend most of their time in the shallow end of the relationship pool, never venturing into the deeper water of commitment and genuineness.

Because of the need in all of us to know and be known, it's essential you spend time reflecting on your own life and the impact you can have on your grandkids. That way, you can give them a taste of what deep and genuine relationships look and feel like. This essentially means that you must continually review the things in your life that may push them away. Look at the log in your own eye rather than the speck in the eye of your grandchild. You'll never be able to address the speck if the log is blocking your vision. Nor will they let you.

I've found there are some ways of engaging with teens that shut them down and push them away. I tell parents these parenting styles are somewhat antiquated. For grandparents, these can be relationship ruiners.

I've never heard a mother say, "I want to have a perfect daughter." I've never heard a dad say, "I'm going to rule my home with an iron fist. It's either my way or the highway." I've never heard a mom and dad say, "We want to be judgmental parents."

But I have heard hundreds of young ladies say, "My mom wants me to be perfect." I've heard hundreds of young men say, "My dad is so strong-headed and authoritarian I can't wait to get out of the house." I've heard thousands of kids say, "My parents are the most judgmental people I know."

This applies to grandparents as well. Because guess where most parents picked up these antiquated styles of parenting that are no longer effective and, honestly, are quite abrasive? From their own parents, most likely. Yes, from you. Ouch! Hurts to dig that log out of your eye, doesn't it? But it's essential if you want to maintain a desperately needed relationship with your grandchildren.

Where does the disconnect come from? If parents and grandparents long to be loving, forgiving, and grace-filled, but kids often see them as critical, negative, and strict, who's right and who's wrong? Or is it a matter of right and wrong at all? Are you all on the same team?

Let me explain the common complaints I hear from teens about their authorities.

They Demand Perfection

Perfection (or in a Christian home we often call it *excellence*) is an easy ask of grandkids in their early years. We want to teach and model perfection, as Christ is supposed to be made perfect in us. (See Hebrews 10:14.) Most young kids really believe the world is ideal, they are awesome, and their parents are textbook picture-perfect. As they enter adolescence, everyone (including themselves) falls right off the pedestal. Their eyes are opened to a world that isn't as great as they thought and people who aren't nearly as perfect as they hoped. Disillusionment sets in.

One of the major changes in a child moving into adolescence is the switching of their mind from concrete to abstract thinking. Their perception of the world increases, and their concept of perfection changes as they get zits, hair, and other grown-up parts. They get made fun of, experience rejection and disappointment, question their existence and don't feel like they belong.

Many times, encouragement from adults now feels like a demand for perfection. Questions about grades are taken as insults for not making all A's. Comments about weight or the need to watch what you eat are interpreted as you saying they are fat. Remarks about being on the cell phone all the time are taken as barbed innuendos that they are rude. When they lash out in frustration shared, it is often misdiagnosed as disrespect when they really don't mean to be disrespectful.

At the beginning of the adolescent years, teens and 'tweens (as kids enter adolescence earlier) are fragile and sensitive. They can appear ambivalent, unsure, uncertain, indecisive, doubtful, and torn as to which path to take. At a time in life when they feel the most imperfect, it is not wise for a grandparent to hold up a banner of perfection. Set the bar of expectation and achievement too high and they won't think they can meet it. They'll become either anger-filled as they beat themselves up trying, withdraw into unhealthy habits or friendships, or give up and shut down or push you away.

Simply put, do you like being around people who are perfect? Or think they are? I don't. A condescending and arrogant presence pushes me away. It's fake and disingenuous. I prefer the presence of imperfect people who allow—no, who welcome and embrace—other imperfect people. Your grandkids do too.

They're Too Authoritarian

Parents and grandparents have God-given authority to parent kids. God placed kids in your life for a reason and a purpose. He placed grandkids in your life for a reason and a purpose. He placed you in their life for the same. How we communicate and use our position makes all the difference in the world to our grandkids.

Here's an example. I believe a policeman has achieved a position of authority in society. However, the way this officer of the law approaches his role makes all the difference in the way people respond to his authority. If he is relational, most people will respond accordingly. However, if this policeman comes across as a strong authoritarian, he will probably push more people away than gather them around him.

They may have to bend to his authority, but they don't have to like it—or him.

You are in the same position. How you exercise your authority determines if you draw grandkids to you or push them away. It's not that the authoritarian approach is wrong. It just doesn't work any longer because of the changing climate of the adolescent culture. Overall, American culture no longer respects people in authority or positions of authority. It's not hard to understand why culture turned in this direction. Just reflect on what they hear about pastors, police officers, politicians, coaches, teachers, and others in authority. Stories of the abuse of power are most of the focus. While I think many of these perceptions are erroneous, I understand that perception is *truth* to the one who perceives it.

Perception is *truth* to the one who perceives it.

That means whether I like it or not, whether I think it's right or wrong, the authoritarian approach to grandparenting doesn't work. That doesn't mean you give up your standards or compromise your values or faith. It just means a different angle can be much more effective with teens than a heavy-handed approach.

They Come Across as Judgmental

Here's one we're probably all a little guilty of. Remember, it's how we are perceived by our grandkids. This determines whether they think we are judgmental. It's all about perception. In today's politically correct culture, being judgmental is a pretty sensitive topic.

When you talk about race, homosexuality, couples living together, divorce, teachers, police officers, or any pet peeves (like I listed mine in Chapter 3), how do you come across to your grandchildren? To the world? Is there a hint of judgment in your words or tone?

Not many years ago, we were able to say whatever we wanted. We used plenty of words that weren't politically correct, and other expressions that today would be considered rude that we thought were kind of funny. When I'm with trusted friends, I can say what I want and express thoughts I would never say in front of my grandkids. That's because the world they are growing up in doesn't tolerate a hint of judgmental attitude toward anyone. It's not at all funny to them.

Is it right or is it wrong? It doesn't matter. If my grandchild feels like I'm judgmental and that is getting in between our relationship, no matter how much *freedom of speech* I have or how wrong they may be in curtailing my right, I stop. I cherish this special relationship, and I don't want to do anything to damage it.

My grandkids are not just grandkids; I want them to be my brothers and sisters in Christ. I don't want to do anything to make them stumble.

In order to counter the above ineffective ways of engagement with teens, I preface my comments. I use statements like these at the beginning of many of our conversations, just so they know my intent.

- I don't want you to be perfect, but how do you want me to…
- I don't want to be pushy, but you're putting me in a difficult position by…
- I don't mean to be judgmental, but help me understand what is going on here.
- I know we're all imperfect, and I don't mean to come across as a know-it-all.
- I want to hear you, but I want you to hear the heart of what I say also.
- I know we think differently about this, so help me understand your view.
- Do you think age has something to do with our perception of this?

By prefacing what I want to say, I steer them away from thinking I demand perfection, act too authoritarian, or judge too much.

How do your grandkids perceive you? What would they say about the way you come across? Would they say you demand perfection? Would they say you rule the roost? Would they say you rule the family kingdom with an iron fist? Would they think you are somewhat judgmental?

Ask them. Text them and ask. Call them and ask. Don't be too chicken. I double-dog dare you.

Perhaps say it this way:

"Sweetheart, do you think I want you to be perfect?"

"Hey, do you feel like I come across pretty harsh and immovable sometimes?"

"I need to know something. Do you think I'm a judgmental person?"

"If you could change one thing about me, what would that be?"

"What is one thing about our relationship you would like to be different?"

Whatever their response, let it sit for a while. Then let them know you'd like to get together and talk about how you are preventing your relationship from growing. Let them know how much they mean to you. Make a pact always to clear up, address, and discuss anything that might come between this special relationship God has placed in your lives. You'll be so glad you did.

Chapter 8

Being a Superhero When Their Lives Suck

My message and my preaching were not with wise and persuasive words, but with a demonstration of the Spirit's power, so that your faith might not rest on human wisdom, but on God's power.
1 Corinthians 2:4-5

When Maile was sixteen, she texted me one time, "Poppa, can we get together for dinner? Just us?" I quickly responded that as soon as I got back in town from a speaking event, I would pick her up and we'd go wherever she wanted to eat. "Yes, Sweetheart, in a heartbeat," I replied.

You know what? She just wanted to talk. Not really about anything remarkable or astounding. That wasn't her point. She was really asking, *Am I valuable and important enough that you'd like to get together?* I heard it loud and clear and quickly responded "yes."

One of these days, she'll ask if we can get together again, and it will be something remarkable, maybe earth-shattering. I'm convinced those critical conversations will never occur unless I'm willing to invest time in the smaller conversations that build trust and affection first.

Many times a grandparent is just the attending ear that listens and listens and listens and listens. When you're through listening, you listen a bit more. Somewhere in the midst of wearing your ears out, a grandchild begins to believe you're a superhero. All because you showed up and engaged in the nick of time.

They'll remember your stories and bits of wisdom, just as you and I did growing up from the adults who spoke to us and into us. From my early childhood up through my thirties, I was like a sponge soaking up anything I could to figure out who I was, what I was supposed to do, and what my purpose was in life. It might not have taken me so long if the voices I heard in my elementary and teen years encouraged more than discouraged. My sponge soaked up quite a bit of negative from people who were more critical than wise.

When you're through listening, listen a bit more.

Even after I became an adult, many other adults I knew spent time telling me what I couldn't do rather than what great things might be in store for my wife Jan and me. People said I shouldn't have dated Jan as long as I did. Some said we shouldn't have gotten married so early. We've now been married forty-two years. Some folks close to me said I shouldn't work for a church. I worked on a church staff for seven years. I met many parents who thought I was constantly wrong. In fact, I couldn't do anything right in their eyes. Many said moving to Branson, Missouri, to work for Young Life was a mistake. We spent seven years at YL as well.

The biggest punch in the gut was when a fellow sat with me and told me he didn't think I was capable of starting Heartlight. He thought it would fail if I tried it. He thought moving to Texas was going to be a big mistake, and he stated I just wasn't capable of the plans I thought God had for us. In a way, he was right. I wasn't capable, but God was. He knew my calling, my passion, and my purpose. He created me for it.

The people described were naysayers, people that always saw the glass half-empty and who took one-way trips to Negative Town, always emphasizing the worst of any situation.

I've said for years that it's not the presence of negative comments but the absence of positive comments that set one's life on its course. The positive for me came from older folks in my life who chose to sit with me and listen. All times of the day, any day of the week, they could be counted on to listen to my hopes and dreams, offering input only when I wanted it or asked for it. From them, I learned some important lessons that came from their ability to use experience and knowledge to make good decisions and judgments. Wisdom flowed from conversations. I'm sure they never realized the impact they were having on me. As I reflect on their effect on me, I guess their influence was what a grandparent could have offered me.

I've spent a lot of time looking back on my life, thinking about those people who helped me become who I am. As I try to imagine what I would be without their words of wisdom, well, I just can't. Most of these guys are dead now. Some have lost their spouse. Others have lost their mind. I still keep in touch with a few. All of their legacies live on in me.

When I worked as a youth pastor at the church in Tulsa, a fellow named Dave Tillack told me, "Mark, don't stoop to be a king when you're called to be a servant." Think about that one. For me, that was a totally different perspective than being told to put others ahead of myself—the same principle, but a new way of hearing and perceiving it.

The pastor of that church, Dr. L.D. Thomas, and I were out for lunch at the Tulsa Oil Club one time, and I remember him pointing to everyone in the room, saying, "Mark, every person in this room feels like they're carrying the weight of the world on their shoulders." Another pastor there, Doug Burr, told me a number of times, "Mark, God's going to use you."

I remember the renowned author and speaker Chuck Swindoll saying, "Everything that has come to you has first passed through the hands of God."

John Roberts, a swim coach I had for a number of years, said, "Mark, if you think you can, you will. If you think you can't, you won't. For many, a race was lost before the gun even sounded."

Smith Brookhart, a dear friend in Branson, Missouri, would remind me, "Markus, you're doing a good thing."

Spike White of Kanakuk Kamp, who took me under his wing, would say, "Mark, have you thanked the guy who fired you and brought you to Texas?"

Pete Herschend, another dear Branson friend, would say as we started Heartlight, "Mark, remember that your revenues will always be half of what you expect, and your expenses will be twice the amount you planned for."

Wishard Lemons told me when talking about ministry, "Mark, people in ministry don't laugh enough."

Joe Mooberry once said, "Mark, most Christian ministries cater to women; it's our job to serve up a good meal to men."

Cliff Taulbert shared with me over coffee, "Mark, you've got to be genuine, and you've got to be real, or people won't stand to be around you."

A lady named Margo Dewkett, who taught me about breaking horses, said, "Mark, how you treat a horse when you're on its back is pretty much how you treat those people that live around you."

All of these folks probably don't even know the impact each simple-but-wise sentence had on me. I'm not sure I knew how important they were at the time. In hindsight, I see how each molded me and how God used them to influence me. It was these guys (and gal) that left a legacy of hope for me. To each, I am most grateful.

It's interesting how each of the comments I remember these superheroes of mine making didn't use scripture. However, each undoubtedly stood on biblical principles for their own lives. Sometimes, wisdom is shared from the ways you internalized God's Word in your life. You naturally express it through golden statements based on your experience and knowledge.

In all their time with me, each of these people had similarities in their influence that presented a wonderful example to me. Now I can use my influence, in the same way, to share wisdom with my grandchildren. You can too. There are a few common practices to note:

1. These one-liners didn't come out of just one meeting. They were nuggets I remember from a span of time we spent together. Conversations didn't set out to solve a specific problem at a specific time. They were just ongoing conversations over a long period of time.

2. These friends were intentional about training me. These meetings weren't just to shoot the breeze or pass time. They recognized they had a sponge sitting there soaking up anything it could. They were purposeful (not agenda-driven), with a desire to pass on something that would make my life different.

3. Time spent together was positive. At least, it seemed like it was. I'm sure they said things that needed to be said, but I always left our times together with a sense of encouragement, not discouragement.

4. Each gave room for me to ask questions, millions of them. They weren't afraid to tell me answers I didn't want to hear, but they told them in an affirming way. I trusted them when they were right; I trusted them when they were wrong.

5. These steadfast *rocks* had insight, meaning they processed their own experiences and drew out insight and wisdom to be passed on to others.

6. They told stories. Their own stories of successes and failures, challenges and hurdles, and what they had learned or picked up in the process.

7. No matter how I saw something, each always helped me see things from another perspective.

8. Deep down, I knew each of these folks loved me and enjoyed the time we were able to spend together. I felt their

commitment when they introduced me to friends, other colleagues, and folks we would bump into during our times together.

9. They didn't spend time correcting me by telling me how I needed to do something different, now or next time. If they did, I think I would have checked out and put them in the same category as other naysayers in my life.

10. They acted as a remedy, helping me figure out God's best for my life.

I'm sure you can list a very similar group of people that influenced your life. I bet you can list what each person taught you. Well, now it's your turn to be that influencer, storyteller, perspective-giver, sharer of successes, communicator of failures, insight injector, and positive trainer. God placed your grandchild in your life for a reason. He also kept you in theirs for a greater purpose.

You've had plenty of years to have the light shine on you. Now it's their turn.

Chapter 9

How a Place of Retreat Becomes a Haven of Rest

Come to me, all you who are weary and burdened, and I
will give you rest. Take my yoke upon you and learn from me,
for I am gentle and humble in heart, and you will find rest for
your souls. For my yoke is easy and my burden is light.
Matthew 11:28-30

Recently, I sat in a living room with a crowd of people who had come to see two older folks, grandparents who had gotten up there in years (each in their nineties). Four teens were in the room and some fifty something siblings. Everyone listened as these two oldsters told all their medical stories of the previous six months. We all heard about hemorrhoids, calluses, bunions, bum knees, poor eyesight, hearing loss, something getting burned off, urine samples, and the need for another colonoscopy, endoscopy, and polyps removal. Getting old is not for the faint of heart.

I sat there trying to figure out how I could find a fork somewhere in the house and give myself a root canal to make the whole experience a little bit more pleasant. The four teens didn't utter a word. They were speechless after hearing all the graphic talk about the various health challenges. The rest of us periodically nodded and said, "uh-huh," "okay," and, "Then what did the doctor say?"

It was two hours of misery and gloom. As I suffered through it, I couldn't wait to get out of there and away from the discussion I really had no interest in. Am I exaggerating here? Maybe just a bit, but not far from the reality of that scene.

We may all be in that position one day when medical issues are about all we have to talk about. (I hope that day is a long way away.) I left thinking I never wanted my grandkids to feel as uncomfortable around me in my home as those teens did sitting around listening to the shocking realities of getting old. Then I started thinking how I do make some people feel just as uncomfortable in other ways.

My grandkids tell me I'm always cleaning. My daughter tells me I need to learn how to relax with messiness at my home. My son-in-law tells me that I can't always have everything perfectly put away. My wife says I'm obsessive-compulsive. You know what? They're all correct in their assessments. I can make anyone feel uncomfortable because there is something in me that always cleans. Always.

Guests become paranoid whether they put their dishes or cups in the right place, and family is always concerned I'm watching to make sure everything is properly stowed. If someone is missing something, they come to me first. They know I've probably thrown it away if it was just sitting around.

I have to work hard to keep my need for cleaning and picking up clutter from getting in the way of relationships within my family. I can only imagine how many times my kids and grandkids have looked for one of their belongings because they put it in the wrong place. Well, to me it was the wrong place. So I felt compelled to move it to the right place. They had to get used to my idiosyncrasies.

Many times, the way you want your home to be can keep your grandkids from being able to kick back and relax when they come visit. Your mission, should you choose to accept it, is truly to make your home their home. It should be a place of rest, a place to kick up their feet (yes, even on your pristine, glass-top coffee table sometimes) and consider it their second home.

Jesus said, "Come to me all who are weary and heavy laden and you will find *rest*." He didn't say, "Come to me and you will find a way to give yourself a root canal." He said *rest*. I can't think of any group of people who deserve a place to rest, a place of sanctuary, more than your grandkids. They go out and do battle every day against a world that works against what

> The least we can do is give them a place to recharge.

they and we desire for their lives. They fight a contrary culture trying to steal their morals, values, faith, relationships, health, and peers. The least we can do is give them a place to recharge.

They're worn out. They're beat. They need a break. They need some rest. They need a retreat. They need a place where they are heard and listened to. They need a respite that refreshes and invigorates. They are looking for a safe harbor amidst the storm where they can refuel and be understood. I hope your grandkids find that in their own home, but it's never a bad idea to be the backup plan, an extension of love and grace found in your—the grandparents'—home.

I want that to be your home. I hope you do too.

Let me ask you something. What do your grandkids feel when they walk in your front door? Is it a place where they find the rest they need, or is it a place where they are more worn out by the time they leave? Do they tell each other stories behind your back, quietly making fun of the way you do things? Is it a place of avoidance where you know everyone will only get along if there is no talk of politics or religion?

Will they bring their friends to meet you? What do they sense from you? Do they feel welcome? Is there always an open invitation? Would they spend the night with you? Do they sometimes just want to hang out with their grandparents?

There are a number of ways your home can provide a setting for physical, emotional, and spiritual rest. These include the setting you design, the atmosphere you create, the rules of operation, and the conversations your home invites. Let me explain.

Setting

I bet your grandkids would love to come to your home and find a place warm in relationship, relaxed in its furnishings, and welcoming to every weary and heavy-laden teen. Like a favorite restaurant, they long for a place where they can be catered to if you will.

I've walked into many a home where everything was in such order and so clean that it made me look messy! These homes feel like sterile environments that couldn't possibly allow the smallest amount of dirt or mess to enter its doors. I mean physical, literal mess or emotional and spiritual clutter. No controversial or messy talk would be found here. For teens, the welcome mat might as well say, "Don't cross this threshold."

I've walked into homes where families are so concerned about how everything looks on the outside that teens feel like their *dirty* insides better not come anywhere near it. Performance and appearance reign supreme, sometimes even at Grandpa and Granny's house. This kind of home is so concerned with how everything looks that little attention is paid to what's happening inside the heart. As long as grandkids look great on the outside, all is well, even if they're falling apart on the inside.

When they were young, you probably taught your grandkids to put away the games, toys, puzzles, and dolls they played with, right? Told them there is a place for everything and everything in its place, encouraged tidiness and supported the 1880's phrase *Cleanliness is next to godliness*? Admit it, did you ever tell your grandkids the myth that a messy room means you have an unorganized mind?

Are you still saying things like, "Square it away," "Straighten it up," "Keep it in order," and, "Clean up your room"?

Well, if your home is an extension of who you are, then what message is your home communicating to your grandkids? What message are your words communicating to your grandchildren? What phrases do you say the most with them? Are you sending a message that says they have to have their lives in order, put together, straightened up, clean, tidy, and everything in its place to be with you? Or do you give signals that your home and you are a safe harbor where your grandkids can be a mess, fall apart, and be less than altogether?

I think they prefer the latter because it offers a hand of hope. That kind of message says, "You can fall apart here; messes are welcome." Which message would appeal to your teen grandchild?

Hey, I know about cleaning and having everything in its place. Believe me. So I have to work hard to create a haven that welcomes anyone who is a little disheveled and in disarray. My wife has a pillow on our sofa that says it wonderfully, "A Beautiful Mess." She puts it there just to bug me, a hard-to-miss reminder to me to quit cleaning.

Atmosphere

The setting has more to do with the physical attributes of your home. The atmosphere has more to do with you. From the moment your grandkids knock on the front door to the time they drive off, you create the atmosphere.

Jan and I own a timeshare in Cabo San Lucas, Mexico, where I am writing this book. It's our second home, a getaway from all the hustle and bustle of travel, speaking, and living with sixty high school kids. I love this place. I love the food. I love the activity. I love the beach. I love the people. I love it all, except for one thing—the way that they greet me within five minutes of getting out of the taxi. Someone inevitably asks when they can meet with me so they can sell me something or push their agenda on me. It grates me. It's not the way to start a relaxing time away from home.

> From the moment your grandkids knock on the front door to the time they drive off, you create the atmosphere.

When your grandkids walk in the door, who is the focus of attention? Their first interaction should not be about what you want or planned, it should be about them and what they want.

If you only see your grandkids a couple of times a year, might I suggest that before they enter your home, you have some type of communication throughout the year? That way, they know that you have an interest in them beyond a couple of weeks at Christmas or during the summer.

I'd like to suggest some ideas that might help create the atmosphere you want, to help them engage in the setting you create in your home.

- Build a fire pit in your backyard and create a place for conversation (not lecture).
- Sit around a fireplace more.
- Get tickets to a concert that your grandkids would like to attend and take them.
- Have a few good jokes to tell around the dinner table that will bring some belly laughs or tell some old stories that will bring people to tears.
- Get that larger flat screen television and purchase whatever is needed to play some video games.
- Get a trampoline and put it in your backyard (for them, not you).
- Get a golf cart for your grandkids to drive around.
- Have plenty of board games to invoke fun and conversation, not *bored games* hated by all.
- Work on a thousand-piece jigsaw puzzle of a picture they like.
- Cook the meals they want.
- Have a refrigerator full of their favorite foods.
- Get up early and have a wonderful breakfast awaiting them.

Don't have your music, your TV shows, your schedule, your favorite food, and your plans for games take over. Don't sit around and talk about your next medical procedure. This time is not about you. Remember, you only have so much time with your grandkids until you either kick the bucket or their calendar gets full and de-emphasizes your role in their life. You have one shot during the teen years as a grandma or grandpa. Make it count!

A word to the wise: Don't just have activities to fill the time. If your grandkids come over and you take them to a movie, remember they can see a movie anytime. They only get a small amount of time to see you. Make memories.

Above all, create an atmosphere where they know they are safe. A good friend of mine reminds me every time I see him that Jan and I are safe in his home. That is such a relief. It gives us permission to be ourselves, speak what is on our hearts, and share any concern or frustration that may be on our minds. It's an atmosphere that can only be created through relationship.

Rules of Operation

Okay, so I know many of you have read this far and probably think I advocate letting the crazies run the asylum. Just put the kids in charge and everything will be fine. You may think I promote just letting the grandkids come into your home and do whatever they want. Not at all. I believe in rules to construct the boundaries and limits, so all can function within a relational environment.

Grandkids need to understand what is allowed and what is not allowed in your home. These rules are necessary. You may even need to put up a small blackboard or sign that says, "Grandma's House Rules." When expectations are clearly stated, they can be correctly met. Everyone knows what's going to get them in trouble and what won't. Kids can still make either good choices or bad choices at that point, but they should know beforehand the limits and the consequences. Talk them out so you don't get taken advantage of when you can't hear or see them, or when you fall asleep before they do.

Here are a few rules I would include in your list:

1. Everyone and everything will be treated with respect.
2. You are always welcome here. Anything illegal is not.
3. This home will be a safe place for all. Don't think you are the only one here.
4. Bedtime is midnight. House is locked. TV, tablets, cell phones, game systems, laptops, and any other electronic devices are off.

5. No use of cell phones during meal times; video games limited to one hour.
6. If your parents have different rules, we support and follow them unless they make an exception for your visit.
7. We will share anything with your parents we think might be dangerous to you or others.
8. We don't expect to be taken advantage of. We don't owe you anything, but we want to give you everything.
9. No rudeness, crudeness, or nudeness, and don't kick our dog.
10. We can talk about anything; just keep it courteous.
11. You must understand there is nothing you can do to make us love you more, and there is nothing you can do to make us love you less.

Conversations Your Home Invites

Technology doesn't solve problems or create deeper relationships, conversation does. Good meals, a welcoming atmosphere, and a relational setting all work together so you can have conversations that offer opportunities to share your wisdom and give hope to your grandkids.

Another shift in the way grandparents should act is to allow a conversation that reveals the messiness of life, your life and theirs. You need to shift the focus from expecting excellence to allowing for failure. Welcome their imperfect selves and imperfect lives and their imperfect teen world to integrate with yours. Stop resonating perfection. They are old enough now to know nothing and no one is perfect. Anyone who expects perfection is a hypocrite or a fake.

Remember, I mentioned earlier (Chapter 7) how a teen needs to be in the presence of imperfect people as they begin to realize and comprehend that their once-perfect world is just not anymore. Grasping this is tough. It's sad. And, yes, it's messy.

Making imperfection more comfortable is essential. "For all have sinned and fall short..." (Romans 3:23, KJV) now becomes a reality.

Teens can more than relate to what Paul wrote to the Romans when he said, "For I do not do the good I want to do, but the evil I do not want to do—this I keep on doing" (Romans 7:19).

This is not the time to be quoting to your teen grandchild, "Be perfect, therefore, as your heavenly Father is perfect" (Matthew 5:48). That will only discourage, not encourage.

Admitting imperfection is really pretty easy because you have never been perfect. No one is this side of heaven. Confession is the key. It makes you relatable to your teen grandkids. This should happen in the form of sharing stories of struggle, failure, disappointment, and hardship. Tell your grandkids when it was hard to forgive and easier to hate. Tell them how you handled it when someone picked on

Your imperfect conversations open the door for your grandchildren to talk about their newly discovered imperfections.

you. Tell them your biggest disappointments and what you later learned from them. Unfold the conversations at natural intervals, in short stories on walks, during games, in the car—not lectures but doing life together. Your imperfect conversations are essential to open the door for them to talk about their newly discovered imperfections.

Your words affirm their struggle and give them hope that they too can overcome the struggles and difficulties they face in their teen years and beyond. Your words help them identify with you. Your shared experiences connect you.

A young father of four once told me after attending one of our seminars that the day his dad admitted failure and showed himself to be imperfect was the day hope was ushered into his life.

I can tell you this for sure. Your grandchildren don't care as much about your accomplishments as your stories of disappointment. Your accomplishments may motivate; your stories bring hope.

So be careful of your words and how you come across. The setting, the atmosphere, and the rules of your home create a pathway for a conversation that is open and raw, vulnerable and bonding. In his 1960 book *The Four Loves*, author C.S. Lewis lamented the opposite of such an atmosphere in families at times and affirmed the power of positive words from parents and grandparents alike.

> We hear a great deal about the rudeness of the rising generation. I am an oldster myself and might be expected to take the oldsters' side, but in fact, I have been far more impressed by the bad manners of parents to children than by those of children to parents. Who has not been the embarrassed guest at family meals where the father or mother treated their grown-up offspring with an incivility which, offered to any other young people, would simply have terminated the acquaintance? Dogmatic assertions on matters which the children understand and their elders don't, ruthless interruptions, flat contradictions, ridicule of things the young take seriously sometimes of their religion insulting references to their friends, all provide an easy answer to the question, *Why are they always out? Why do they like every house better than their home?* Who does not prefer civility to barbarism? (Lewis, 42)

Your home will one day be silent. The chaos of kids and grandkids will be gone. Time moves on and so will your family. My hope for you is that everyone's memories of your home will be of rooms full of love, a kitchen overflowing with great scents, and walls that echo laughter. I hope your home is a place of fun, hope, relaxation, and safe harbor for grandkids that know that they know that they know your deep love for each of them.

Chapter 10

Touching Their Hearts When Their Behavior Hurts Your Heart

*And we know that God causes all things to work together
for good to those who love God, to those who
are called according to His purpose.*
Romans 8:28 (NASB)

My son's phone call was expected. His message was not. "Dad, I'm getting divorced," he said.

The neighbors could hear my response, I'm sure. "What do you mean, you're getting divorced? You just got married! What are you thinking?"

"I've met someone else," my son said.

I remember telling him, "Well, Adam, when you can call your wife's father and apologize for screwing up her life, then I'll talk to you."

Doesn't that sound great? Wasn't it manly? I thought I was doing the right thing, standing up for what was right. I was defending what God desires and what we stood for as a family. I said that to my son as well. Mind you; this was the same son who inspired the tagline of truth I've communicated to hundreds of thousands of parents—*There's nothing you can do to make me love you more, and nothing you can do to make me love you less*. Now I wasn't so sure.

When my son needed me the most, I wasn't anywhere to be found. While he was lost, I let him wander. When he needed a dad who would walk with him through a difficult time, I wrote him off. During this difficult time, my presence in my son's life was lacking. Then I woke up one morning and realized what I thought I was doing in the name of righteousness wasn't working. The more I thought about it, the more I came to see how I put my expectations above my own son. I justified my behavior with the idealistic thoughts that I was doing what God wanted me to do. Boy, was I wrong.

Adam hurt me. When I turned my back on him, it was because of my own feelings. I was thinking more about myself and how I was going to lose a daughter-in-law that I loved than I was about my son's turmoil. I did not consider the internal conflict and struggle he was going through. Yep, I put myself first.

Just today I had a salesman tell me, "I like finding out where other people are wrong, and I love having them say I was right." His comment was exactly how I responded when my son hurt me.

I've spent hours of reflection since then looking in the rearview mirror. I believe God would have me spend more time trying to touch the hearts of those who are hurting me than protect my own heart or convince myself I am protecting God's very own heart by turning my back on any one of His precious kids.

A father of one of the kids who lives with us recently let me know he was disappointed in me. I wasn't standing up to the media and publicity he felt were exploiting his daughter. She was engaged in a same-sex relationship, and the media loved revealing this scandal. The media exposure defamed him, his wife, and Heartlight. The media were relentless and started making accusations that our program was into *conversion therapy*. They tried to paint Heartlight as something we are not.

Eventually, I decided it would be best for this man's daughter to leave our program. It wasn't working for any of us. The media exposure portrayed Heartlight falsely, and we could not find a good resolution in the situation. I also thought that publicity could bring problems to other families and teens entrusted to us at that time.

This father and mother are dear people. They love their daughter immensely. Asking them to come pick her up from our program was hard on them and me, but the choice I had to make was in the best interest of the Heartlight program. The father caught me somewhat off guard when he said, "This approach is not what I would have expected. It gives the impression of fear, not confidence in the Lord's provision." He felt we should fight not only for his daughter but also against the homosexual agenda. I disagreed. That is not Heartlight's mission. I just didn't think that was our fight.

His comment got me thinking quite a bit about what stand we are supposed to take when we encounter people and situations that don't follow what we believe. Scripture says the following:

> But you, man of God, flee from all this, and pursue righteousness, godliness, faith, love, endurance and gentleness. *Fight the good fight* of the faith. Take hold of the eternal life to which you were called when you made your good confession in the presence of many witnesses. (1 Timothy 6:11-12, emphasis added)

I believe the fight mentioned here means fights and quarrels that get us up caught up in arguing over things that create nothing eternal. Matter of fact, I further believe this scripture is pretty targeted at encouraging people to fight the good fight that pursues righteousness, godliness, faith, love, endurance, and gentleness. All these things are eternal.

I don't think this scripture means I am to fight everything that doesn't line up with God's Word. Hey, I'm not looking for a fight. My grandkids get beat up enough from peers. I don't want to look for a brawl in which there is always one winner because that also means there is a loser. I don't want to be a loser. I sure don't want my grandchild to think he is a loser either.

I also don't think this scripture tells me I must fight other people's battles. Some people really believe it is their job to create or finish any and all fights. I don't. Some admirable and honorable battles just aren't my business. If I spend all my time trying to fix all the cultural and political issues around me, I doubt I would have any time to develop relationships. Love might get lost in the fight. I am called to love on people the way God directs me to do so. When I love on them correctly, and we develop relationships, then I can step into a fight for them or fight with them, rather than fighting against something. When that happens, we both win. There's nothing wrong with fighting for a cause. It's just that some of those causes aren't mine to fight.

So, where does this come into grandparenting?

You are getting older. You have things you believe in and a number of things you don't believe in. There are things in this world you don't agree with, and probably there are many things you downright despise.

As this new and changing culture emerges, don't confuse love and listening as acceptance. No one is saying you have to embrace what you believe is sin. It's just that sometimes (I would argue most times) we need to let the Holy Spirit be in charge of making those we love *accountable* for their sins. That's the Spirit's job anyway, isn't it? Who made it ours?

Be careful. It's easy to get caught up in some of the quarrels and controversies that are more about fighting than they are about resolution. Maybe the way you believe is different from the way your grandchild believes. You can spend the time fighting, and both lose relationship, goodwill, and love. Or you can love in spite of the differences in your beliefs and still be able to listen and impart your stance without offense and without losing your special relationship.

Here's what the Bible states right before that verse about fighting the good fight:

They have an unhealthy interest in controversies and quarrels about words that result in envy, strife, malicious talk, evil suspicions and constant friction between people. (1 Timothy 6:4-5)

My message is simple. Don't fight for something that produces nothing. Don't engage when it only produces anger and destroys relationships. Instead, fight for the relationship with that special person God has placed in your life when you encounter differences of opinions, no matter how big or small.

Don't fight for something that produces nothing.

Some situations may be hard to swallow, but they may also be the biggest opportunities to show how much you love your grandchildren in spite of your differences. I encourage you to think about these possibilities before you are faced with any of them, so you don't react negatively when you find out what's going on. Think about these now, so you can keep your head on straight if any of them occurs within your precious family.

You have to figure out how you would respond when you first hear that your grandson or granddaughter is gay.

You may have to accept the fact that your grandson is living with his girlfriend, and you'll have to figure out how to love him even if you don't approve of the living situation.

You will probably have a grandchild who thinks it is okay to smoke pot. Will you let the difference in how you feel about something that has no eternal value determine (or destroy) the relationship you have with your grandchild?

If you differ on politics, the changing climate, or same-sex marriage, do you think you can share wisdom about these hot topics when there is disagreement on the particulars?

Can you still participate and attend a grandchild's wedding if the couple is already expecting a baby?

Can a discussion about transgender bathrooms and same-sex marriages produce a perspective that your grandson or granddaughter has never seen before?

Can you still love a grandson or granddaughter who sees nothing wrong with smoking, gambling, drinking, or other violations of your standards?

Will your granddaughter still feel the specialness of the relationship with you if she is just a little immodest and parties more than you ever would have wanted?

Can you continue to love your grandchildren if they marry people you don't like, approve of, or think are not the right spouses for them? Will you still be involved in their lives in a way that leaves the legacy God designed you to leave?

These scenarios are easy to read on the page, much harder when they hit home. When any of these scenarios happen within *your* family, what will your reaction be? Hopefully, these situations are not just sprung on you, but are preceded by a few conversations and time for you to give wise (and sensitive) input when it counts the most. You have an opportunity to help form opinions and beliefs, rather than just being a recipient of your grandchild's announcements or a bystander watching behavior you think is inappropriate.

Your relationship is key. The God of relationships calls you to be a light in the darkness and a beacon of hope. Your words of encouragement can be a rudder that steers even the mightiest of ships to a different destination, or a spark that lights up the darkest of nights.

You may think, *Okay, how do we do that, Mark? How do we approach a subject or situation that is contrary to what we believe without alienating our grandchild? What do we say? Will our grandkids even listen to us?* Great questions.

First of all, yes, they will listen to you, but only if you have already established a solid relationship where you are a trusted source of wisdom. If you haven't built the relationship, then I doubt you can come in and share your opinion and make much difference. Without relationship, giving unasked-for advice creates more distance. Chances are, your grandchild already knows what you believe regarding the situations I listed above. They are fighting mighty internal battles. They already fear they disappoint you. They already worry you will condemn them.

If you won the right to be heard with your presence throughout their lives, yes, I believe they will listen.

Your approach to your grandchildren at critical times shows what your relationship can withstand. More than you think, I promise. However, what you say and the tone you use set the course for ongoing input and interaction.

If your grandchildren live close to you, it will be easier to communicate on a regular basis. Grandkids who are geographically distant present more of a challenge. If you only get to spend time together a couple of visits a year, it becomes a little trickier. In that situation, you may want to invite them to go on special trips, vacations, or weekend expeditions. FaceTime or Skype as often as you can. Make sure you find the time to talk.

As your grandkids reach their teen years and beyond and you need to talk about something tough, I'd approach the discussion by saying, "You and I know I'm old, and I don't see things in the same way perhaps much of the world accepts. We're different, you and I, but we have had and always will have a special relationship. Right now, I want to speak to the *elephant in the room.* Tell me what's going on in your life. I want to know what you're thinking."

That should get you in the door to have the conversation. Remember to ask questions. Whatever the answer (however misguided in your eyes), ask more questions. Hopefully, after you spend a period of time of listening, your grandchild will ask you something along the lines of, "What do you think?"

Be careful here. I find sometimes it just isn't a good idea to share your opinion. Many times I look at kids when they ask that question and say, "It really doesn't matter what I think. I'm happy for you, and you know I'll never let any of your decisions get in the way of our relationship."

There's a scripture that states,

Fools have no interest in understanding; they only want to air their own opinions. (Proverbs 18:2, NLT)

That reminds me to wait when I am asked for my opinion. I

need to consider first, *Am I being a fool? Do I want to understand my grandchildren? Did I really hear their hearts, or was I formulating my own counter arguments the whole time they shared?* Sometimes my opinion is just not needed. Other times it may instill a sense of disappointment in my grandchild.

Let me ask you this. Once you hit your teen years, didn't you know your own sin better than anyone? Did you hide things from parents or even trusted friends? If anyone *caught* you or *condemned* you for your choices, did it help? Most of the time, teens know exactly what they are doing wrong in their lives. In fact, often they feel worse about themselves than they really are. They feel worse about their mistakes and failures than you could ever make them feel. If they are making poor choices in some areas and have been *brought up better*, then they most likely already think the ones they love see them as utter failures, not just human beings who mess up sometimes. They don't need to hear it. They need to be loved and encouraged through it.

That verse in Proverbs directs me at times to simply respond with, "I understand." They may say, "So you're okay with me doing (whatever it is they are doing)?" My response is, "I didn't say I agree with you. I said I understand, and we can still love one another and not agree with everything you're doing."

> I can still wholeheartedly love and embrace a grandchild who doesn't want or take my advice.

If I sense my opinion or perspective will be ignored at that time, then I don't share it. That's like casting pearls before swine (not that I'm calling my grandkids pigs, although I'm chuckling on the inside as I write this). You know what? I can still wholeheartedly love and embrace a grandchild who doesn't want or take my advice.

One big key to parenting and grandparenting is *don't take it personally*. After all you have tried to teach and instill in them, their sin and poor choices can certainly feel personal. When your grandchildren hurt themselves or damage their lives or the lives of others, of course, it hurts you. It hurts badly sometimes. But you can't make your hurt the focus, or you will lash out in ways that won't be welcome. Put your hurt feelings aside for now. You're the grown-up.

I encourage you first to let parents handle some of the confrontations and deal with the conflict that arises when a grandchild makes seriously bad choices. It's the parents' fight. Your role is to encourage the parents (your kids) when they need it, let them know you want to come alongside them and help (not interfere), and be that safe place your grandchild can come and feel like they can discuss anything. Anything.

Because you've no doubt already experienced more than a few times when your own kids hurt your heart, you can handle situations with your grandkids a little differently. Where you missed it with your daughter, you can be right on with your granddaughter. Where you screwed up with your son, you can do better with your grandson. In a way, grandchildren give you a chance for a do-over. Take full advantage of it.

Oh, and my son Adam? He married again, as did his ex-wife. He married a girl he loves dearly, and my ex-daughter-in-law married the man of her dreams. They both posted on Facebook the same day announcing the birth of their kids. Out of the thousands of Facebook friends I have, their posts were listed right underneath each other. What are the chances of that?

It was almost as if God was trying to tell me that regardless of circumstances, and regardless of whether I understand or even agree with them, He does work all things together for good. He uses pain to create passion and purpose. He makes your mess into your message. He takes tests and turns them into testimonies. He did it for my son and for me. I stand witness to how He does it for thousands of teens who spend time at Heartlight. You can trust He will do it for your grandchildren and you.

Chapter 11

When Health Gets in the Way

And surely I am with you always, to the very end of the age.
Matthew 28:20 (NIV)

As I wrote this chapter, I was talking with my granddaughter Macie. "You know one day I'm going to kick the bucket, don't you?" I said.

She said, "Kick the bucket? You mean croak?"

We laughed, but as I looked into her eyes, I saw the reality of that truth. One day, I'm going to be leaving this little girl. I answered her, "Yep, but hopefully not soon!"

"I hope not, Poppa, I hope not," my Macie said.

When your first grandchild is born, you realize how fast life is moving. You are getting older. A new generation begins, and another eventually ends. Becoming a grandparent is the first signal to us that the aging process will not be passing us by.

I think the second time in life we recognize the passage of time is when we lose a parent. We realize we are slowly creeping to the age where wills, burial plots, retirement, health care, and legacies are more on our minds than ever before.

We also think about our mortality when we begin to have health issues. When a doc looks at you and says, "This is what you have," it's difficult to hear the diagnosis partly because it reminds us one day we will be gone. Sometimes that reminder rattles us more than the actual health issue.

Maybe the hardest marker is the loss of a spouse. After years of being together, the hardest act of love is letting go of the hand of your mate and placing it into the hand of God. The lonely times of loss intensify thoughts that you may be next in line. Grief looms heavy, the price you pay for love. During this time, it is important to take advantage of the precious time left in life to secure your legacy as a grandparent in the hearts of your grandkids.

All of these things have a remarkable way of getting us to think about mortality, don't they?

I have a kidney disease inherited from my mom. She died from it, my grandfather died from it, and my aunt died from it. There's no prevention, and there's no cure. The only hope of not dying from this ailment is a kidney transplant, which just means I will die from something else. No matter what cure is found for whatever disease, there's always another to remind you you're going to die from something. The stark realization that this life on earth will one day end is something no one escapes.

When I first heard I had polycystic kidney disease (PKD), I immediately changed my diet, worked out more, changed my lifestyle, and did what I could to prolong my life for as long as possible. I think my main motivation for the lifestyle changes was to make sure I wouldn't leave soon. I don't want to leave soon, even though I know the grim reaper always shows up earlier than expected to the dinner party.

I'm really not afraid of death. At least, I don't think I am. What I am afraid of is how it is going to happen. Chances are, it's not going to happen in an accident. Knowing that, I still wear a seatbelt in the car and a helmet when I ride horses and motorcycles. For me, it will probably be a slow death from a disease where I will have time to prepare how I'll leave, if not exactly when I'll leave.

Before my mom died, she never wanted to talk about death. I'd visit her in the hospital and at the nursing home, and she would not even broach the subject. I'm not sure if she was scared of death or not willing to accept the fact that she was going to be gone one day. Because she wouldn't accept it, she never had the opportunity to say the things she needed to say to those who loved her. She died within minutes of being told she was going into hospice, probably scared to death (literally) at the thought her time had come.

I think we should look at major health issues another way. Take advantage of them. Put them to good use as reminders that life is short, and the time to leave a legacy is right now! If dementia or Alzheimer's doesn't set in too soon, some health issues give us the opportunity to make amends, call and make things right, and say our final goodbyes.

The inevitability that my life will end motivates and fuels me to want to leave something behind. It pushes me to be very intentional about how I spend my precious minutes, and how I speak to and treat those around me. The inevitability of death makes you laugh more, take advantage of conversations, be bolder when you say what needs to be said.

I don't want to be like my mom. I don't want to ignore the inevitable and miss out on the opportunity to share the things deep in my heart, the truths and nuggets of wisdom I learned. My mom's passing didn't motivate me to look at my ancestry and make sure that my affairs were in order; it motivated me to look ahead to the end so I can take advantage of every opportunity before me now. I want my grandkids to remember that I had open and honest conversations about life, from the beginning of our relationship to the end.

Be very careful, then, how you live–not as unwise but as wise, making the most of every opportunity. (Ephesians 5:15-16)

I think the wise person, if capable, utilizes every opportunity God allows to leave something behind that can affect the lives of his grandchildren. I don't want to wait until my last day on earth when I'm drooling all over myself or taking my last breath. When I realize it's my grandchildren's last time to hear from their Poppa and my time to wrap it up with the hard goodbyes, I will give assurances they'll be okay and tell them I'll see them soon. I want to usher in hope 'til the very end.

Utilize every opportunity God allows to leave something behind that can affect the lives of your grandchildren.

I don't think the last words you say are the most important words of your life, a crescendo, with wisdom just waiting to come forth. I've been around plenty of people who are dying and what they say at the end is not the most significant. My mom's last words to me were, "Mark, your mustache is so white." That's it? The most important thing she had to say was that? Are you kidding me? The most important words said in a person's life are the ones filled with wisdom and shared over a period of time to children and grandchildren. Most flash-in-the-pan, end-of-life comments will be soon forgotten, but a life well lived will never be disregarded.

I believe the significance of a life can be seen in the words of those who surround the one who is dying, as they reflect on that person's influence.

I knew a man named Smith Brookhart for more than thirty-five years. When I turned thirty, he turned fifty. All I wanted for my thirtieth birthday was to eat dinner with him. We did. When I turned forty, he turned sixty. Again, all I wanted for my birthday was to eat dinner with him. We did. The same happened when I turned fifty, and I asked for the same when I turned sixty. It happened each decade until I turned sixty. My schedule was crazy, and his health was failing so we only talked by phone. We laughed about the possibility of eating dinner together on my seventieth. We both knew it wasn't going to happen.

A heart transplant extended this dear man's life as far as it could. Diabetes weakened him, walking became difficult, pain racked my friend, and ten years of health issues took their toll. Smith and Gail, his wife of fifty-six years, could see the end of the road. They knew Smith's eternal destination of heaven was not far away. They kept their sons Chip, James, and Tom up-to-date on every part of their dad's health.

The family shared updates and reports with all who asked, including the grandkids that spent most of their life with a Poppa who had health issues.

In spite of his failing health, Smith's responses to the cards he had been dealt were nothing short of amazing. Each morning he would list ten things he was thankful for that day. His welcoming demeanor, his warm hugs, and the way he would say each of his grandkids' names upon their arrival to his home changed their lives. Gail, "GG" to her grandkids, shared how he tenderly loved the grandkids (and really everyone) with jokes and smiles, even in the midst of his battles with health. He loved to laugh and kid around. He made others feel good even when he didn't feel good. Smith and Gail continuously expressed thanks, feeling blessed with more than they deserved.

Amazingly, he continued to be a Poppa, to love on his grandkids and influence each of their lives in spite of his major health problems. This strong ol' ox wasn't going to let a failing heart, failing kidneys, and failing body keep him from failing as the Poppa his grandkids expected him to be. He fulfilled his desire to maintain his role of influence and encouragement in their lives.

Smith was a calculating man, a banker by profession and a bean counter by design. His precise logging of his sugar levels amazed the doctors at the Mayo Clinic. His meticulous scorekeeping of Saint Louis Cardinals baseball games impressed all. He expressed his reasoned responses with authority, his opinions with discernment (most of the time), his faith with conviction, and his compassion with thoughtfulness. His sons knew this well. His grandkids saw him as a hero, almost larger than life itself.

In spite of his frailties, he witnessed to others about the Lord, and a couple dozen folks commented how they strengthened their walk with God as a result of seeing Smith wander through this maze of health challenges.

The last ten days of Smith's life were spent in a hospital. When his kidneys started to fail, the family members called, Skyped, and flocked to his bedside to say goodbye to their Poppa. He had been up front and honest about his condition, and he shared the reality of his dying as much as he shared about living. This brave man imparted to his grandkids many things they will never forget.

Smith knew that time on earth is short. He understood that upon receiving a new heart, he was living in *overtime*, in extended play. That's when he dedicated his remaining days to be part of his grandkids' lives. He spent time talking about everything that was happening with him. At the very end, it was not his last words that meant the most, but all he gave throughout his life. Smith lived and died well. He knew the memories he etched on the hearts of his grandkids would have to suffice once the life he shared with them was over. The grandkids' memories of this man speak loudly to the impact he had on their lives while battling failing health in his.

The grandkids' memories of this man speak loudly to the impact he had on their lives while battling failing health in his.

His grandson Stewart said, "What God did with Poppa was the same thing that Michelangelo did with a frayed imperfect piece of stone. He took it and created the beautiful masterpiece, *David*."

A few months after his Poppa died, young grandson, Everett said, "You know, I really miss Poppa. I love coming here, but it's not the same. Can we get a substitute?"

An older granddaughter Casey shared, "He was incredible. Every time I walked into a room, Poppa welcomed me with a loving smile and voice, saying, 'How's my Casey Ann?' That would make me feel special. He was very intentional about conversations, very interested in what we were learning, and not always wanting to teach us something. He loved us, encouraged us, and I think of him quite often, mostly when I'm in his house with GG. He was the most patriotic man I know. He loved people and loved Jesus, and let us know how important that was to him by the way he lived."

Grandson Parker said, "He didn't make a big deal out of his health stuff, so most of our discussions were just normal. We all knew that we were going to lose him soon, but he kept on going as if everything was okay. Even when he felt bad, he made us feel good. Whenever I think of Poppa, I think of tough love. I think of Poppa all the time."

Granddaughter Allison stated, "Poppa was full of determination, intentionality, and paid attention to detail. He wouldn't hesitate to be a part of our lives, even when he wasn't feeling well; and he let us know! It never kept him from coming and being a part of our lives. When I had my last conversation with him, I let him know that I was fearful of him leaving and not being at my college graduation, or meeting his great-grandkids, or being at my wedding. His response was that life on earth was fleeting; just a vapor, and soon we will all be together again. He told me he was grateful to be a part of my life and assured me that I was going to be okay. I was never more proud to be his granddaughter."

High school graduate Smith IV shared, "Poppa is probably still the greatest role model I know. When I look at the way that he lived life, even though he was going through pain, he still loved all of us. He wasn't going to let his pain get in the way of relating to us all. I think a lot about the last time I hugged him. But the thing that I remember the most is how Poppa loved me, cared for me, and listened to all that I had to say."

When eleven-year-old grandson Anderson got on the phone to tell his Poppa goodbye for the last time, he said he needed to be brave, just like Poppa showed him.

The common thread that ran through each of these grandkids' comments was how Smith, their beloved Poppa, made them all feel special, a theme each grandchild felt and knew in his or her heart.

The death of a grandparent is often a grandchild's first experience of watching the end of the cycle of life. That's why the experience has such an impact on kids. Watching a grandparent with health issues is real life. It can be seen, understood, and felt. Having a grandparent die feels surreal, a new experience that transitions a child from concrete to abstract thinking. Death is foreign, unusual, strange, and surreal because it is not a common experience for them. The definition I like of surreal is *unearthly*. When a grandparent has health issues, it's earthly. The minute death comes, it moves to something heavenly and unearthly.

That being said, an important aspect of managing health issues with grandkids is helping them understand. Have those comments and discussions that prepare them for life to end one day. When you get sick and have health issues, don't hesitate to help a grandchild come to an understanding of what's happening with you.

Help your grandchild feel like hope is not lost, but your passing will be hope fulfilled.

Toward the end of your life, it's also important to give them assurance. Assurance that all is going to be okay, that you're going to be fine in the arms of Jesus. Help them see that, as you have trusted Christ with your life, they are going to have to trust Him as well when you leave them. Help your grandchild feel like hope is not lost, but your passing will be hope fulfilled.

Health issues (sigh).

They have a way of disrupting our plans and maybe ushering a new plan you never anticipated. I know this. However, it's not how people perform when they are well that speaks to their character. It's how they respond when they're not doing well that speaks volumes about their true strength and integrity.

Smith Brookhart IV said, "I'm going to remember this about Poppa—how much he loved me, how much he loved our grandmother, and how much he loved our family."

That speaks volumes to the influential role and determined, intentional desire my friend Smith had to leave an impact on his grandkids. Two of Smith's grandkids ended with this, and it's how I hope we are all described by our grandchildren long after we are gone. *Poppa fought like a warrior to be with us so we would all get to know him.*

And fight my friend Smith did. He fought to influence his grandkids to walk in a manner that is worthy of God, and to love family like there's no tomorrow.

What are you doing to leave that same kind of legacy?

PART III — YOUR LIFE'S WORDS

Chapter 12

Giving Your Grandkids
What They Want

Tell your children about it in the years to come,
and let your children tell their children.
Pass the story down from generation to generation.
Joel 1:3 (NLT)

In case you haven't noticed, teens communicate differently today than we did when we were teens. The Internet ushered in a new way of not only communicating, but also finding information, answers to questions, instructions to live by, entertainment that never quits, and new ways of social networking. Teens may think they are making tons of friends on the World Wide Web. They may feel like they are communicating with the whole world. However, the reality is that talking, making friends, commenting, and meeting on the Internet isn't the same as talking face-to-face, sharing meals, getting together, and hanging out. These newly found Internet *relationships* many times lack real involvement and investment in one another's lives.

Internet posts on just about any social network depict lives that are idyllic in appearance and performance. Conversation is more about the transfer of information, a *daily diary* of what one is doing communicated through pictures and hashtags. It's mostly one-sided, a scream for attention, and self-satisfied when all the *likes* and superficially pretty comments come rolling in.

I'm not saying all the impact of the Internet is bad. I believe the good from it far outweighs the negatives that are given much more attention. But the way teens communicate begs for deeper interaction, and grandparents have the perfect opportunity to fill the communication and connection gap most teen grandchildren feel.

To understand the need for your involvement in the lives of your grandkids, it's important to understand the world of communication and cultural influence they live in. You need to know what you're fighting against to make sure your intentional message of leaving a legacy isn't lost in the white noise surrounding your grandchild.

A Culture of Negativity

There's a benefit to filling out surveys, writing reviews, stating opinions, and reflecting on experiences. There's something to be said for critiquing services, rating the performance of a business, or sharing a perspective or opinion on just about anything. People want to be heard, and the Internet now provides a way to speak, regardless of whether or not anyone is listening. Quite honestly, I think it will remain part of our culture for years to come. The negative side of this effort to rate every business, every politician, and every service is we have become a world where too many consider themselves *judge and jury*.

Given time, anyone can find fault with anything. There will be a bad meal served at a restaurant that has served thousands of great meals. There will always be mistakes, shortcomings, disappointments, and unmet expectations as long as man is alive. If you look hard enough and deep enough into anybody's background, you can find faults, discover disappointments, learn about their mistakes, and obtain information that can be misused to trash them. The negativity of the culture has exploded. People are critical, complaining, yelping, rating everyone's performance, and sharing opinions publicly. Everyone now has the *right* to complain and the ability to put those complaints out there on the

Internet for the world to see.

People do have the right to complain. But it doesn't mean they should. To me, constant complaining counters the first verses of Matthew 7, which state,

> Judge not, that you be not judged. For with what judgment you judge, you will be judged; and with the measure you use, it will be measured back to you. And why do you look at the speck in your brother's eye, but do not consider the plank in your own eye? (Matthew 7:1-3, NKJV)

Today, we live in a culture that considers negativity just *being real.* The problem with negativity being the norm lies in the fact that it creates an absence of positive messages to counterbalance the constant stream of bad stuff. In other words, so much time is spent focusing on and explaining the negative that little time is spent clarifying and illuminating anything positive. Teens don't hear positive anymore. They hear where they failed, didn't measure up, and what they need to do better next time.

An Atmosphere of Know-It-Alls

Secondly, this culture of negativity is filled with know-it-alls and self-proclaimed authorities who really believe they've cornered and mastered certain roles because they've tried or experienced something once or twice. Sharing personal experiences becomes a platform interpreted as wise and authoritative merely because it is videoed, blogged about, or printed.

I don't write this book based on what I learned from being a grandparent. I am a grandparent of four, but that hardly makes me an expert when it comes to helping folks connect with their grandkids. What gives me the platform to speak on grandparenting is my work with thousands of families. I have seen firsthand the significant impact, and ways grandparents are indeed creating a legacy of influence for their grandchildren.

I recently watched a video of a young lady who has an autistic son. She shared the ways she thought everyone should handle their autistic children. I've seen plenty of videos and blogs of new fathers sharing what they are learning about fatherhood. They have infants, and they are already online telling everyone else how they should parent. Suddenly, these new dads are the experts. I've seen and listened to many who adopted one child. Now they evidently know how to counsel everyone else on how to raise an adopted child. It's like everyone has suddenly become experts because they have a platform where they can share. A blog is practically viewed as a doctoral degree, allowing just about anyone to think he is a specialist because of one experience.

That's about as sensible as calling me a veterinarian because I helped a vet sew up one of our horses who had a deep cut. Or call me an obstetrician because I delivered my own son. Maybe I'm a preacher because I spoke in a pulpit. I'm not a dentist just because I brushed my teeth this morning.

Sharing one's perspective does not make a professional. Her own personal story alone does not give the writer or blogger the credentials to lead others. As grandparents, we know this because we've been around the block a few times and understand that just because you see something or read something doesn't mean it's automatically the truth. It does not mean it is totally accurate either. It's just one person's perspective based on what they saw or felt.

Teens are falling hook, line, and sinker for many people's foolishness because they know no better. They interpret information as wisdom. They can hardly tell the difference between the two.

Two things happen when everyone is a know-it-all or a so-called expert. One, it creates a world of false wisdom. Two, it inflates many people to believe they know more than they really do.

Hey, I can change spark plugs in my car, but I'm not a mechanic.

A World of Fantasy

Third, a world of fantasy existence combined with geographical contentment has captured many teens. In plain English, that means many teens and even young adults are happy to stay holed up in their bedrooms posting their observations, hopes, and a whole lot of selfies on social media rather than go out and engage with the real world. They remain where they are rather than moving forward to a better situation in life. Change takes self-discipline and drive, and they don't have any to help them improve, grow, and mature. They use social media posts and affirmations as validation they are doing great, when in reality they may not be.

Here's an example. I recently saw a post on Facebook where a young lady stated she finally feels content with her life. She found new confidence to face everything before her. She stated she used to be goofy with her words, crazy in her actions, and immature in the way she related to people. She added that she used to view her appearance negatively, but now is satisfied and pleased with where she is.

I was excited for this young lady that she developed newfound confidence in herself. Then I read the comments of all her *friends*, and they alarmed me. All 110 of them affirmed everything this young lady said she was feeling. That sounds great on the surface, but the truth is, the young lady still struggles with many of the issues she now thinks she *used to* have. In their desire to stay on trend, the friends' comments completely skipped over the truth. Now I don't think Facebook is the right forum to *speak the truth in love*, but if this young lady takes these comments to the bank, she may not take steps to progress in the ways that will help her succeed in real-life situations.

Truthfully, this lady is a wonderful young lady. But she is obnoxious. She is goofy to be around. She acts crazy at times. She's very immature for her age. If she doesn't work to make some changes physically, she'll likely face serious health problems in the future. The oh-so-encouraging comments addressed none of these issues. Again, I am glad no one called her out on social media, but if she counts on social media as her only belief system, will she accept truth from anywhere else if it's hard to hear?

There needs to be someone in this young lady's life who speaks the truth so she can become better, reach her potential for deep relationships, find significance, and go places to use her gifts and talents. Contentment quickly changes to complacency, and motivation to move to a better place gets lost.

I said earlier it's not the presence of the negative, but the absence of the positive that causes a problem. Let me add that inundating youth with shallow positivity and no healthy motivation also damages. Hearing only positive comments to the point of pretending nothing negative exists sometimes hurts more than it helps.

It's not the presence of the negative, but the absence of the positive that causes a problem in a teen.

This new culture is difficult for teens to navigate. On the one hand, the cultural tone (political, doom-and-gloom attitudes about the climate, gender wars, left vs. right, and more) is so negative it has teens worried, walking on pins and needles about their futures. False information from so-called experts leads them to second-guess what they hear and read. People commit horrific acts like rape and murder and broadcast them live on social media. On the other hand, teens' social media circles go overboard in their praise of what is sometimes patently ridiculous.

It's like that old children's fable of the emperor and his new clothes. At the end of the story, the emperor marches through the streets naked, foolishly convinced he is wearing fine garments. Even more foolishly, his subjects all pretend he is fully clothed too. They praise the beautiful new outfit the emperor wears, and he is stark naked as a jaybird.

Even though teens want to believe it, fake affirmation causes them not to trust what they hear, wondering whether they are really being told the truth.

This cultural struggle provides a perfect setting for grandparents to enter. In a world of negative, know-it-alls, and half-truths, your grandchild is looking for a positive, trustworthy speaker of the truth in love. Your voice of tried-and-true experience can rise above the white noise that drowns out sensible and wise advice. That's your call. Will you accept it?

You can be a voice in the darkness of this world that gently offers what your grandkids are searching for desperately. Speak truth, whether they seem like they are listening or not. When they hear something completely different from those around them, but they're not quite sure who to believe, your history with them of love and support can convince them you're the one who's telling it straight.

Giving Your Grandkids What They Want
(Even When They Don't Know They Want It)

Recently when I was traveling, I stopped at a well-known burger joint inside the airport. I ordered a cheeseburger (medium rare, no onions) and fries. With anticipation, I awaited what I understood would be the best burger ever. However, when the waitress brought my order to the table, the hamburger was burned to a crisp, there were onions everywhere, and they brought onion rings instead of fries. I didn't get what I wanted.

I told the waitress, and she said they'd fix it. Fifteen minutes later they brought out a medium-rare hamburger with no cheese. There were fries this time, but I still wanted a medium-rare cheeseburger. I told the waitress I ordered a cheeseburger, and I still didn't get one. She apologized, took the plate back, and vowed to get it right this time. Third time is the charm, right? Not in this case. The third time around, I got a medium-rare cheeseburger with fries. The only problem was the onions on the burger. I still didn't get what I wanted or ordered.

I said thanks, promptly took all my belongings and left. I had no time to get another meal elsewhere. My flight was about to depart. I didn't get what I wanted. I felt frustrated. I was still hungry as I got on the plane. At that point, I wanted to eat anything. I had to settle for airline snacks because the place I had anticipated disappointed me greatly.

I expected something satisfying. When it disappointed me, and I didn't get it, my hunger pangs drove me to settle for something far less than what I really longed for. My hunger got satisfied, but not with what I wanted. Now every time I see that burger joint, I remember the failed cheeseburger experience and I turn away. My sense of disappointment remains, not only in the burger place but also in a waitress who really had no interest in taking care of my order or me.

This scenario reminds me of the scripture from Luke 11:11-12 that says,

> Which of you fathers, if your son asks for a fish, will give him a snake instead? Or if he asks for an egg, will give him a scorpion?

In this scenario, if the son doesn't get what he wants, eventually he'll leave and go elsewhere so his hunger can be satisfied. Grandparents can give grandchildren a satisfying meal of wisdom when their culture and social circles offer them an *incorrect order* of foolishness. Teens are asking for *fish* and *egg* to fuel their lives. Often they're given only cotton candy, the *fluff* of information overload, instead.

Grandkids don't come to grandparents to get more information. They usually come to ask questions. They are seeking insight and direction. This offers the perfect opportunity for you to share your mistakes, failures, and struggles. After all, they are the source of much of your wisdom.

Quite honestly, information is a dime a dozen. It can be found anywhere and shared by anyone. Google, Siri, or Alexa can provide facts and details. That kind of stuff is not what your grandchildren are looking or hoping for. Again, they are looking for wisdom, the ability to use experience and knowledge to make good decisions and judgments. Information is communicated in the teaching model; wisdom is shared in the training model.

One of my greatest concerns for teens today is how many are viewing scripture as information, not wisdom. Because they're in an information world, they categorize scripture as just another historical reference, a good story, more material to process, a mere set of data that is part of their family tradition.

What they want to know is how scripture relates to them. How can the Bible help them get to a great place in life? That's the wisdom from the scriptures, but it needs to be presented in a way that seems applicable to their real lives. Grandparents can share that.

For example, scripture clearly states sex within marriage is the only form of sexual relations of which God approves (Hebrews 13:4, 1 Thessalonians 4:3, Jude 7, Colossians 3:5, Galatians 5:19, 1 Corinthians 5:1, 2 Corinthians 12:21). For many teens, this is just information from a dusty document. How does it work today? Why would it make sense to swim against a very sexualized culture, when sex is fun? Why should teens deny themselves when everyone else is doing (and flaunting) it?

Here's where they need wisdom—the wisdom you have and can give. This wisdom is more than repeating the scriptures they already know. This wisdom explains why this principle should be followed. It gives practical examples of the benefits and drawbacks of following the culture or following the Bible. A grandparent might communicate the wisdom packed in these verses in the following way:

> "In all my years, I've heard and lived by the same principles my parents taught me. This is what I found. Sex before marriage has an unbelievable way of causing confusion in relationships. So, if this is the girl you're going to one day marry, make sure you work hard not to confuse the relationship. Work hard not to 'muddy the waters' with the one you will spend the rest of your life with."

This sample conversation includes not only the truth and information they've been given but lets them hear the importance of this principle. It emphasizes how it is relevant to them. In a world of information bombardment, can you dig deep and give them wisdom? When they ask for what they want, give it to them in a way that equips them to counter what the culture offers. Help them leave your table of conversation satisfied, not hungry, so they won't accept phony substitutes or shallow facts to satisfy their longings.

This wisdom is usually shared through stories of failures, successes, and lessons learned. These transform information into a true-to-life experience that can affect their choices and selections in life. Share your wisdom with intentionality. Don't just blow smoke in their ears. You don't tell the stories of your life for the satisfaction of telling them. (Remember the old folks who detailed their health ailments and scared their grandchildren and me away?) You tell them to offer a balance in their unbalanced world. You tell them to speak the truth in love, with affirmations of good and encouragement to mature in areas of much-needed growth.

This wisdom is usually shared through stories of failures, successes, and lessons learned.

The Art of Storytelling

Most times, wisdom and hope are shared through stories that include a concept or nugget of truth that sticks in your grandchildren's minds because the stories give them something they want.

Do you tell good stories? Can you think of the funniest moments in your life? How about the most bittersweet? What did you learn from the best and worst times of your life? What memories bring a smile to your face? What tales could grab the attention of your grandchild as you sit around the dinner table or in front of a fireplace talking? Your life stories help your grandchild get to know you better, but they can also help them examine their own lives in light of the choices you made.

Surely you have plenty of stories you can weave into *morality tales*. A morality tale is a story with a lesson of right and wrong. Make sure each of your stories has a punch line of truth, a lesson to be learned that they will remember. Don't overdo it. Often, just one line is enough. Make them think and leave them wanting more.

Making kids laugh is wonderful. It's a true gift when you can attach a life truth that you gathered and now want to pass along. Earlier, I mentioned a comment made to me that changed my life. A dear fellow named Dave Tillack told a story. Then he said the infamous line (for me it was anyway) that stuck with me.

"When you're called to be a servant, don't stoop to be a king," Dave said.

I don't remember the story, but I will forever remember that one line.

Some of the most impactful stories I tell teens are the ones where I share my own humanity. I admit my mistakes and struggles. I reveal my vulnerability. I've learned to pull the humor out of all those stories, and I aim to keep it to one point per story. Ten lessons in one tale either wouldn't make the tale very interesting (more like a lecture) or too hard to take in and apply. (Why waste all those great things teens need to be taught?)

Practice your stories, even out loud in front of the mirror. Think about the funniest comedians. They take real-life situations and bring out the extraordinary. They admit when they acted foolishly or saw other people do something silly. They practice these routines again and again. Then they perform them over and over, honing and perfecting their craft. The best comics leave us wanting more by bringing their humorous anecdotes back around to something more serious. They leave us with a heartfelt lesson they learned. We love their routines because we can relate.

Think back over your life. Jot down some stories or say them into a voice recorder. Play them back and listen to yourself. Are they funny? Do they come across judgmental? Do they have a subtle message? Try your stories on your spouse or kids and tell them you want to share them with the grandkids. Gauge their response and weight their input carefully. You can leave a legacy of life lessons shared in the most entertaining ways. That's what I try to do with my own grandkids. I want my grandkids to say, "Remember when Poppa told us about...?" Or, "Hey, Poppa, tell us the story about..."

I find most truths transfer best through stories, ones that are unique in origin and simple in approach. A story is easy to remember. Share yours. Include a point but don't give it away too easily. Let them figure out how it applies to their own lives.

Every grandparent has stories. The ones that make a difference offer a point or purpose, packed inside a good dose of humor and transparent vulnerability.

The Intentionality of Sharing Wisdom

I'm convinced sharing wisdom doesn't always come naturally and doesn't transfer just by *hanging out*. Grandparents must choose to be intentional in order to impart something special that brings wisdom to lives of their grandchildren.

> Grandparents must be intentional to impart something special that brings wisdom to lives of their grandchildren.

I was on the phone last night with a man who said he was going to hang out with his granddaughter over the weekend. He planned to spend some time with her as this twelve-year-old struggled to handle her parents' divorce. Her school performance slipped, appetite fled, interest in her extracurricular activities waned, and she isolated herself. She wanted to quit the activities she loved.

Her granddad wanted to help her get through this tragic time in her life by hanging out, but this young lady needed some guidance and direction. That takes more than just hanging out. I'm sure she longed to talk about her feelings, learn how to verbalize her frustrations, and know that it's okay to have a hard time dealing with this major loss in her life. Her actions (or inactivity) and attitudes showed clearly she was asking for help and a little bit of hope. This well-meaning grandpa planned to offer a time of activities and entertainment, but trying to cheer his granddaughter up or distract her from her problems wasn't going to fix the big issue in her life or help her process anything.

I encouraged the granddad to spend some time having fun, but also to plan a time to sit down and open the door to share some wisdom. Maybe it could take place at an ice cream stand, a coffee shop, or her favorite pizza place. But he needed to create an atmosphere of connection more than just fun and activity. She needed more than the junk food of hanging out. He needed to offer her fish and egg, the wisdom to sustain and strengthen his precious granddaughter.

When you have moments to sit down and enjoy each other's company, but a larger issue like divorce still needs to be addressed, I would say something like the following.

> "Sweetheart, I know it's tough when a family is going through a divorce. I know it's a little complicated and you have so many feelings inside your head and heart. I want you to know if you ever need to talk to someone who has big ears and can listen well, I'm here for you. We can have fun, as I always do with you. But I want you to know I'm not afraid to talk about the tough stuff that you're going through too. Understand what I'm saying?"

She may not say anything other than, *uh-huh.* But at the very least, in this situation, the granddaughter knows her grandparent is available to listen and offer hope in a situation she considers hopeless. Over time, grandkids come back and share with grandparents who invite them to do so. If you don't offer anything more than a good time, grandkids might believe you only want to keep things light and can't deal with the harder things in life. Or they might feel you love them when all is going well, but can't (and won't) handle them when anything is wrong. Walk the tightrope of conversational wisdom with your grandchildren. If you fall, get back up and try again. Be intentional about sharing the wisdom you possess that can help your grandchildren.

Exposing the Truth in Love

Teens need to hear the truth in a way that does not feel judgmental or cloaked as a demand for perfection. It's a delicate dance. Grandparents need to learn not to gloss over what is going on in their grandkids' lives with total praise and good times together, but also to tread lightly at first when introducing heavy subjects. Give them the opportunity to come to you anytime, and don't push or prod too hard. When you strike the right balance, grandkids feel comfortable having deeper discussions.

Grandparents need to land right in the middle, not an authoritarian who points out every imperfection and not the loving people who see everything their grandchildren do as sunshine and roses.

One point about proximity: if you only see your grandchildren once a year, then those times need to be times of affirmation and encouragement. Listen more than talk, ask questions rather than giving answers, and don't focus on dumping on them or getting everything out in the air you heard they're doing wrong. If you only have a short period of time, you need to build a positive relationship.

If you see your grandchildren quite a bit, then it would be wrong not to mention concerns you have. I want my grandkids to know I'm going to love them to pieces, but I will speak into whatever issue comes up. I'm going to speak about the elephant in the room. Confront the obvious. Push past the discomfort of bringing up what we may never have talked about before. But that can't be my main purpose in being a grandparent. Our roles as grandparents are much more than correction.

When you do speak to an issue, make sure you do so in a spirit of love. Don't talk about sore subjects when you are angry. Most likely they'll still be there once you cool off. Approach tough subjects with the intent to help. You are not in their lives to prove to yourself or anyone else that your way of handling their messes and mistakes is the only right way. You are there to support, encourage, compliment parents in correction, and communicate calm wisdom.

Here are some things you can cross off your list. Phrases like these will only offend and push your grandchildren away:

- You look like you're gaining weight.
- Why can't you do things like your brother/sister?
- I told you so.
- If you only used your head
- Well, your actions aren't telling me anything different!
- You always do this! Or, You never do that!
- I don't think you can do it.

- Did you wash your hair this morning?
- Why don't you have better friends?

All of these are veiled judgments in the form of questions. They may hold truth, but they do not communicate love and acceptance. You can try to retract hurtful statements immediately, but they won't be forgotten. Kids internalize harsh statements immediately. Your apology may be accepted, but the sting remains. If you ever have to explain what you mean, then you should have done your homework and practiced a bit before allowing words of shame to come out of your mouth or in your writings to them.

A well-spoken word counters insecurity, inadequacy, and negativity.

Shame-based comments push teens further into inappropriate behavior they are exhibiting to cover the inadequacy they feel. A well-spoken word counters insecurity, inadequacy, and negativity. It gives values to the one who hears it. Positive words say, "You matter." Choose your words carefully. When words damage and harm, the one who said them quickly gets put on the list of teens' favorite people to avoid.

Here's what one young man shared about his grandfather. Which category did he put his Grandpa in?

"Grandpa always listened to me first. Then he would share a story that made his perspective interesting. He had an unbelievable way of being positive when he was sharing something negative about me. He looked me straight in the eye, and I knew I was loved, listened to, and corrected in a way that made me always want to come back for more."

Wow! That is high praise from a teen. Believe me. Don't you want your grandchildren to describe you in those terms? If so, speak to their issues with a great sense of love. Be intentional about taking advantage of the time you have to share wisdom. Pull them out of their fantasy worlds of social media and into real life. Practice your stories and tell them with laughter and a great message.

You can be the one who counters the culture of negativity. You can be grandparents who bring balance to the off-kilter world your grandkids live in. That's giving your grandchildren what they really want.

Chapter 13

Since Nagging and Lecturing Don't Work, Try Something Different!

My dear brothers and sisters, take note of this: Everyone should be
quick to listen, slow to speak and slow to become angry.
James 1:19

I think you know by now I tend to tell it like it is. So I'm warning you up front. This chapter may step on some grandparents' toes. As the kids say today, "Sorry, not sorry."

It's important to talk about certain communication styles many grandparents employ. You used them when you were parents and continue to use them now as grandparents. I'm focusing on two styles in particular—nagging and lecturing. Stop. Just stop it. They don't work.

Leave the nagging and lecturing to the parents to do in their children's early years. If you keep these bad communication habits when your grandkids become teens, I predict you will destroy your relationships.

Okay, I'm going to make some assumptions here. In most families, grandmothers do more of the nagging, while grandfathers have a propensity to lecture.

Let me set the background for my theories.

Grandmothers love teaching their grandkids. Watching little ones grow, develop, and begin verbal engagement is absolutely wonderful. Grandmas get in the habit of teaching. Kids through the age of twelve need to be taught. It's the right model. Teaching involves repetition, constant questions, continuous urging, and helping with appearance and behavior. Grandmothers do a wonderful job at this. They desire the very best in the lives of their little grandchildren. I venture to say grandmothers get more involved in the lives of grandkids during the first twelve years than grandfathers do. Am I getting myself in trouble here?

Grandfathers love to transfer thoughts, opinions, and the lessons they've learned to their grandkids. But, when grandchildren are young, grandfathers pretty much stay in *let's play* mode. When those little kids turn twelve or thirteen, grandfathers spring into action. Suddenly, their grandchildren need to take more responsibility, start growing up, learn some lessons, and hear about the duties in life. Many grandfathers believe they will miss their window of opportunity if they don't gather their messages together and start lecturing.

Their lectures are meant well, but lectures are talks or speeches given to teach. They work well with groups (of adults, mostly). They can be disasters when focused on an audience of one. A lecture is for teaching, not training. A discussion is by far the better route, where the focus of the conversation is not on what Granddad has to share, but more on what a grandchild wants to learn.

One granddaughter I know described her grandfather as a know-it-all who never wanted to listen to anyone. "He might as well go into a room, look into the mirror, and have a conversation with himself. He needs no one else to talk to," she said. That should not be a grandpa's reputation with his grandchildren.

Of course, I'm sure grandmas lecture at times, just as there are times grandpas nag. Both can take note here.

A Google search of the *Oxford Dictionaries* for the definition of the verb *nag* defines it as: *to annoy or irritate* (a person) *with persistent fault-finding or continuous urging.*

The *Merriam-Webster Dictionary* defines *nagging* as: *to annoy* (someone) *by often complaining about his or her behavior, appearance, etc.; to annoy* (someone) *with repeated questions, requests, or orders; to cause* (someone) *to feel annoyed or worried for a long period of time.*

Grandparents tend to communicate through repetition, which is needed before adolescence but must be transitioned away from when grandkids hit their teen years. What once was an effort to help them through multiple reminders now irritates. In a sentence, some grandparents *tell you what they're going to tell you, then they tell you, then they tell you what they just told you.* And if that doesn't work to get someone's attention or change their behavior or thoughts, then they'll say it again.

I'm exaggerating a little, but you get my point.

A nagging wife [or grandparent] is like the dripping of a leaky roof in a rainstorm. Stopping her is like trying to stop the wind. It's like trying to grab olive oil with your hand. (Proverbs 27:15-16, NIRV)

The nag annoys with repeated requests or orders that might sound like these:

- Did you remember what I told you?
- Did you remember today is your mother's birthday?
- Did you clean up after yourself?
- Do I need to repeat myself?
- Are you listening to me?
- Did you buy a Christmas gift for your brother?
- Did you take care of...?
- Why isn't that done yet?

The nag never stops. They wonder why they get responses like these:

- Okay, okay, I get it.
- Stop! I understood you the first time.

- I heard you the first time!
- No, I didn't hear you. I just wanted to hear you repeat it again. (Insert sarcasm here.)
- You don't need to tell me again!
- I'll get on it when I have time!
- I'm not an idiot!
- You're not my mother! (or father)

You should recognize that these responses are all spoken out of frustration. If they don't snap back at you, a grandchild may instead shut down and shut nagging grandparents out.

This is how teens think when someone continually reminds them of what to do, what to remember, or how to behave. Your granddaughter thinks you believe her to be incompetent and irresponsible. Your grandson thinks you're telling him he can't be trusted to complete a project. Your grandchildren will get the message that you think they are inadequate, immature, and ignorant. Are you trying to communicate that they're not capable of handling what's in front of them? Well, that's the message you send when you nag. That's what they hear.

And you know what? Your grandkids might be incompetent, irresponsible, untrustworthy, inadequate, and ignorant. They're still learning. They're still kids. But bigger kids want and need to do more figuring out on their own. Sometimes they fail. Sometimes they don't handle well the requests put before them. Let their parents deal with that.

I truly believe there is one role for the parents and a different—but in the best cases—complementary role for grandparents. When parents try to take over the role of a grandparent, they forget what their role needs to be in the life of their child. And when a grandparent reaches out of bounds and tries to be the parent, the children miss out on an important relationship unique to the one with their grandparents.

Nagging eliminates influence. Nagging at teens also inspires rebellion. It makes teens vow not to do whatever it is you are nagging about, just to spite you. The more you nag, the less they listen. If nagging becomes the norm, they will eventually write you off. Teens who feel inadequate when nagged will try to get away from those hurtful experiences by cutting you out of all future conversations. You'll miss out on your call to connect with your grandchildren, and they'll miss out on all your wisdom because they've turned you off.

Nagging at teens eliminates influence and inspires rebellion.

One young man described his grandmother as one who always felt the need to focus on the negative. She demeaned her grandkids. She may have wanted to do a good thing by pointing out areas where her grandkids could improve. But her presentation came out all wrong. Her family expected her indictments of them whenever they saw her coming, so they eventually just wrote her off. Sadly, this young man reported his grandmother was such a nag and so negative that no one missed her when she passed.

Teens need grandparents to focus on them, but not only on the parts of them that need improvement. Put your emphasis on the interests of your grandchildren. Extend grace, not condemnation. Nagging focuses on what they aren't doing. Instead, focus on the good things they are.

I think I've nagged about this nagging enough.

If you recognize yourself in any part of this chapter, you have time to change. You're still breathing, so you still have time to try a different approach with your grandchildren. I hope you'll take my words as an encouragement to shift your style of grandparenting from what was effective in your grandkids' early years to a more effective and much-needed positive training model that offers the best of you to the not-so-great in them.

Truth be told, your grandkids probably hate your lectures. They love your stories, but can't stand your lectures. Lectures are ineffective and bore your grandkids to death. Conversations and discussions are two-way streets. No one's eyes should glaze over. Aim for dialogues, not monologues, with your grandchildren.

Remember to unpack your wisdom over time and in many

conversations. Some topics may come up for years. Some may be addressed only once. You don't have to *play the whole deck* in one talk as if you will never have your grandchild's attention again. If one of you were on your deathbed, then I would understand this technique. If not, go easy. I know you want to transfer your sage advice so your grandchildren's world will get better and they won't suffer the consequences as you did. That's a great goal, but it needs to be met over time. Make sure you move from lectures to discussions.

Lecture works well during the teaching phase of your grandchildren's lives. Discussion works better and is much more suited to their adolescent years. Lecturing puts the focus on you, taking attention away from your grandkids. Teen grandkids want someone to listen, not just talk at them.

Teens tune out lectures with the rolling of the eyes, a glance at others in the room (clearly communicating, *here we go again*), or by mentioning other commitments they suddenly need to honor. Lecture works well in the classroom. When your teen grandchildren are with you, they're not in a classroom where teaching should be directed at them. They're in your presence, where training should take place with them. The Christian life is more caught than taught.

Try Something Different

Be brief. I prefer half-dozen ten-minute discussions to an hour-long one. While I wish we could sit down for hours and talk, most teens aren't accustomed to sitting still and being attentive that long. Most have not been trained to be able to do so. When teens walk away from me, I want them to know I was interested in what they had to say, kept the conversation brief so they'd want to talk again, and believe we can think differently and still have great connecting conversations.

Take advantage of the times they approach you. My granddaughter recently came to me and asked if she could work for me. She wanted to make some gas money for transportation. My response was, "Sure. Come talk to me and tell me what you want." When she came over, I just said, "Hey, let's talk about your need for a job."

As we sat down, I asked a different question. "Do you think you'll drink alcohol when you're in college?" I said. I asked the question casually, and she responded easily. We talked for a bit, and I was able to let her know how much I appreciate her opinions. I didn't share mine. After ten minutes of talk, I transitioned the discussion to what she really came over for.

Take advantage of the times your grandchildren come to you and want something. Turn them into opportunities to have one of those short discussions that help you get to know them and the beliefs and values they embrace as their own. I learned years ago I'm not afraid to briefly discuss heavier topics when they want something from me. It may seem like a bit of a conversational manipulation on my part, but it is worth it for the sake of a deeper connection.

Here's a fun way to get interesting conversations going. Have an All-Text Thursday (or any day) Dinner. What in the world is that? It goes like this. Have your grandkids over to eat and make sure everyone has a Smartphone capable of texting. Set up a group text with everyone at the table. Let everyone know via group text that all conversation (I mean every word) will be communicated through texting. No talking. Not a peep out of anyone.

Text everyone when it's time to eat dinner. As all come to the table, have a prayer already written to be texted to everyone. Send the prayer. Then text "Amen." As you hear the notification *dings* around the table, start texting for the potatoes. Next, text for someone to pass the meat. Then text for the vegetables. Have fun texting as the only form of communication for the night. Text if someone can get more tea or water for the meal. Text if someone can bring in dessert. Text and ask if all are enjoying the meal.

Then text the following question, "Hey, what's one thing you'd like to see different in your life?" Remember, you'll get a wide array of responses depending on the age of your grandchildren. But it's a different way to pry open the doors of their hearts and minds. Kids respond frankly via text. They say things they wouldn't say face-to-face. So this may be a way to get them to let their guard down and let you in more. You may be surprised at their answers. Use every creative means and opportunity to find out what they're thinking. Whatever they say, don't give your opinion. Just listen (or at All-Text Dinners, just read). Remember, no talking.

Over time, after a couple of All-Text Thursdays, ask a question that dives a little deeper into their hearts. Ask them, "Have you ever been depressed?" or "Do you know anyone who has thought about suicide?" or "What has been the hardest time of your life?"

You can always follow up and tell them the next time you see them that you'd love to talk about their answers if they want. Don't nag. Don't lecture. Listen to their hearts. In time, they'll begin to ask you questions. Then you'll have your opportunity to give input into their lives.

Instead of Open-Ended Questions, Have Open-Ended Discussions

When I meet people on an airplane, I find sometimes it's easier to talk to strangers than people I've known for years. Interesting, eh? Maybe it's because all things are new. It's interesting to find out about their lives, and I'm all ears to hear their stories. Perhaps trying this technique with your grandchildren would let them know that you are all ears about them. Sit down next to a grandchild sometime, extend your hand for a shake, and introduce yourself. Say something like, "Hi, I'm your grandpa. What's your name?" Act like you don't know where they're from, where they go to school, or anything about them. See what they have to share.

Hey, kids love to talk about themselves. Give them the opportunity. Eventually, they'll circle back and show more interest in you because you show interest in them.

Keep asking questions and just wait for it. Wait for that magical moment when they ask that first question of importance. They'll eventually start asking you more questions that will lead to the discussions you long to have.

Picture it like this: you're on one side of the door of your grandchildren's hearts. They're on the other. Your words push on the door trying to open it. If you nag, the door won't budge. If you insist on making the relationship go your way, it's like pushing the door into their faces. Ouch!

With loving words over time, you find out you weren't supposed to be pushing on the door at all. You should have been pulling, gently tugging the handle with encouragement, love, and words of their value and worth. Soon, you'll find you have to back up because they're swinging the door wide open themselves to let you in.

So when they come around and ask you questions, don't give answers that bring you to a standstill. If you know you won't agree, stop the conversation while it's still pleasant. Answer their questions with a touch of wisdom and leave room to have more and more discussions in the future. If you don't have a good answer to their questions or you're not ready to share one, end your discussion with any of these comments to keep the conversation open-ended and ongoing. You can pick it up the next day or the next time you're able to talk together.

- I need to think about that before I answer.
- You know, I'm not sure, but I'll find out and circle back with you.
- I don't know. Can I get back with you?
- Wow, that's a tough one. I'm not sure. What do you think?
- Hey, I'm interested in your comments about this. Can we come back to it later?
- Man, that's a great question. I need some time to come up with a good answer.

A string of conversations that happen over a period of time has much more impact than one big conversation that tries to answer it all. Believe me, Grandparents, it's not about the answer you give, but the way you engage that matters the most. Engage in the right ways, and as your grandchildren get older, you'll be the ones they come to for answers to the deeper questions of life.

Remind Once and Leave it Alone

This anti-repetition thing bears repeating. If they don't get it the first time you mention something to them, forget it. Don't harp, nag, or lecture. Move on, and let them suffer the consequence. Quit trying to rescue them from any possibility of failure. If it's their responsibility to remember or complete something, let them either remember it or forget it and pay the price. The consequences of forgetfulness or irresponsibility speak louder than your shaming words when they forget. You really only have to say it once. They'll listen better next time, or the time after that, or the time after that. (It takes longer for some than others. That's okay. Button it. Bite your tongue literally if you have to.)

> The consequences of forgetfulness or irresponsibility speak louder than your shaming words when they forget.

Saying the same thing over and over expecting a different result is the definition of crazy, isn't it? Waiting for that magical light to pop on where they finally get it is treating your grandchild like a little child. Repetition makes your grandchildren feel childish, immature, incapable and incompetent, not exactly the message that you want to convey to your grandkids when they are teens.

Asking a question like, "Do you know that it's your dad's birthday next week?" may be meant as a gentle reminder, however, it can come across as insinuating they are too clueless to remember. Instead, ask a question in a way that shifts the focus to yourself. "I don't know what to get for your dad's birthday next week. What are you getting him?" Put the emphasis on yourself. That way, they don't feel like you think they're ignorant and can't remember it is someone special's birthday next week.

Quit Interrupting

The greatest barrier to effective conversation is interrupting. It's just rude. It comes across as arrogance. The second the interruption happens, a message is sent to your grandchild that clearly states your thoughts are much more important than what he has to say. If you interrupt your grandchildren on a regular basis to insert your words of wisdom, soon they'll stop talking to you at all. Interruption pushes grandchildren far away from your presence. Interrupting obstructs engaging. There are a couple of scriptures to guide you, verses that share the wisdom in listening first before answering.

> Everyone should be quick to listen, slow to speak and slow to become angry. (James 1:19)

> Let people finish speaking before you try to answer them. That way you will not embarrass yourself and look foolish. (Proverbs 18:13, ERV)

So let them speak. Sure, they'll stumble over words, repeat themselves, and say stupid things. Nine times out of ten you can guess what their next words will be. You might even feel bored. Still, you need to pay attention. Focus on listening to what they're truly searching for behind what they're trying to ask. They will soon learn that Grandma and Grandpa understand them. More and more, your conversations will flourish because they know the discussions will be on their terms, about their agendas, not yours. Above all, you want your grandchildren to feel honored and respected because you give them your full attention when you listen.

Listen, discuss, and repeat. That's a model that builds close relationships and a lifetime of trust.

Grandma and Grandpa, you don't want your grandkids to think of you as lecturing old nags. If they put you in that category, they are likely to treat you like one—an old nag horse that will be put out to pasture, fed and tolerated, but not paid much attention. I don't think that's what you desire in your relationship with your grandkids.

Chapter 14

Not Every Argument Needs to be Argued

Even fools are thought wise if they keep silent,
and discerning if they hold their tongues.
Proverbs 17:28

We live in a world where people love to argue. It's everywhere! Turn on any news channel and you hear arguing. There are TV programs where the focus of interaction is to do nothing but argue. Newscasters love a good argument because it creates good stories. Teens argue back and forth on social sites. Adults argue their points of view in postings and blogs. Politicians spend their lives arguing for this or against that, and groups of people argue for their rights and their longing to be heard.

Teens fight to feel valued. *Will someone please listen to me?*

Young adults in their twenties and thirties fight to feel validated. *Will someone please listen to me?*

Older folks fight to be heard. *Will someone please listen to me?*

Notice a common thread in these? Everyone longs to be listened to. People master the art of arguing in hopes of being heard. That longing is born from a craving to be valued, a yearning to be appreciated and treasured and cherished. I would argue the underlying thread is the desire to be truly known. It's how we're created, to connect in relationships. It's hard to connect when no one listens.

Arguing flourishes today because people aren't listening to one another. When the art of listening disappears, people choose to quarrel, disagree, squabble, bicker, fight, wrangle, dispute, and feud. It's been that way since the beginning of time. The difference today is we have more tools and electronic gadgets to use to argue. Technology makes arguments more readily available, and the capacity for not listening a little easier.

One group sees things one way, and another sees it a different way. There is something inherent in us to want other people to agree with us. We feel valued when we are in accord with each other. In the same way, we feel less valued when others do not agree with us.

The fight to express diverging or opposite views, usually in a heated exchange, is self-focused. If we are intent on persuading others to share our views at all costs, we are self-centered. It's a one-way street—our way or the highway. When two or more people engage in conversation in this manner, it's nothing but a fight. Consensus can't be gained because no one is entertaining anyone else's views. It's all *me first* thinking, with a goal of the meeting of personal needs rather than the needs of anyone else in the conversation. How does that kind of talk line up with this scripture?

> Don't have anything to do with foolish and stupid *arguments,* because you know they produce quarrels. And the Lord's servant must not be quarrelsome but must be kind to everyone, able to teach, not resentful. (2 Timothy 2:23-24, emphasis added)

Some arguments sound good but are steeped in issues that violate everything you believe and hold to be true. Even so, the people making those arguments deserve to be heard. Why? Because all people need to feel valued, known, and heard or they won't be able to trust and listen to any other view. It may take everything you've got not to hotly defend biblically-based beliefs you hold dear, especially when you feel attacked. However, here's where your gentle answer can turn away anger. Your reasoned responses, delivered in ways that honor and respect the other person, allow them to hear a different belief without going on the defensive.

In a culture where arguments are the norm and resolution is rarely achieved, I suggest arguing isn't the best way to influence. Matter of fact, arguing with teens many times just solidifies their position and justifies their viewpoint.

If you're a grandparent of teens, remember this: Not every argument needs to be argued.

I was with a fellow a few months ago who has been receiving quite a bit of criticism about his views on homosexuality. Adamantly opposed to the homosexual lifestyle, he has been bashed and bruised by some media outlets. Others applauded him for his stance and willingness to *speak the truth* and be a *voice in the wilderness*. He told me stories of what people are saying about him, revealed threats that have been thrown his way, and showed me how vicious people's responses have been to him.

Not every argument needs to be argued.

After listening to what had been happening to him because he stood up for what he believes in, I just sat. He then asked what I thought. Instead of answering right away, I first asked him, "Are you looking for an answer or my opinion?" He opened the door and asked me to give my opinion.

I said, "Dude, you need to shut up. You're only going to get bashed, and you may be worsening the issue, not helping."

He was shocked and replied, "Well, someone's got to stand in the gap!"

I responded, "No, not really. If a gentle answer turns away wrath, then I wonder why your answer is not doing that."

It's because his message wasn't being heard as *gentle*. It came across abrasive, in fact. Maybe he wasn't delivering it in an abrasive way. But today's culture has not only ceased to listen but also hears things differently as well. In a world where everyone is looking for a fight, you have to carefully determine when to speak, when to hush, and when to leave it alone. He might have done better to abide by these words.

Do not give what is holy to the dogs; nor cast your pearls before swine, lest they trample them under their feet, and turn and tear you in pieces. (Matthew 7:6, NKJV)

That's exactly what was happening to him. He based his beliefs on what is holy. The Bible can be seen as his pearls here. But casting them widely into a culture that largely doesn't care to hear it didn't work.

One tool you might use to decide whether to speak is to ask yourself this question first. *Does what I am about to say, HEAL?* What I mean by that is this acronym is, does it Help? Does it Encourage? Does it Affirm? Is it Loving? The young man I was speaking to might have the right beliefs, but his comments evidently were not interpreted as helpful, encouraging, affirming, and loving. As such, they did not HEAL. While well-meaning, they caused more division, as seen in the directly opposing comments and backlash he received.

I find as I get older, I don't want to argue anymore. If someone says something contrary to what I believe, I just let them think what they want and leave it alone. That doesn't mean I don't defend my beliefs if I am directly asked. It just means I don't butt in where I'm not invited. It also means I think my beliefs stand on their own. I don't think I have to defend them. Why? Because I will win more people with my love and genuine caring for their hearts than I will be known as a big mouth.

If people in this culture aren't listening, your arguments for your beliefs won't be heard. When you spend your time and efforts building relationships instead of a platform, then you can speak of your beliefs when invited to within those close relationships. That's when hearts, spirits, and lives are changed. I love Jesus because He first loved me, not because He came marching in telling me everything I was doing and everything I believed was nuts.

Until there is a place of safety established, relationships where people will listen and allow others to be heard, there's no use in throwing your pearls before swine. You got to know when to hold them, know when to fold them, know when to walk away, and know when to run. That's called wisdom.

At any given time, I live with sixty high school kids from all over the country. They are great kids with great parents who are struggling with some pretty substantial issues and behaviors. The teens need a place away from home to address some of the things going wrong in their lives, so they come to Heartlight for a year to sort through issues, hurts, and struggles. We have faced about anything you can think of that has to deal with inappropriate behavior, wrong thinking, poor choices and various lifestyles and backgrounds.

Parents send their kids to us in hopes we can help their teen and give the parents direction as to how to handle their child differently. Many families also want us to solve their extended family problems that have been around for years. That isn't our battle in the war for their teen's heart and life.

Under the banners of standing for what's right, seeking justice, and fighting the good fight, many come to a point where anything opposed to what they believe is grounds for battle. At the very least, many people seem to want to grapple until others understand where they stand.

Many grandparents go to sleep at night feeling they did what is right in the eyes of the Lord when they stood up against their grandkids. They mistakenly believe it's a good thing when they let their teen grandchildren know what is right and what is wrong. They never realize what they are truly doing is alienating their grandkids, not only from them but also often from the truths they are trying to communicate. By wielding verbal swords, some grandparents cut their grandkids down and keep the kids from being positively influenced by them in the future.

Doing what is right in the eyes of the Lord doesn't mean you have to argue anything contrary to scripture. Please hear me carefully here. You should honor God in all that you do. I'm not encouraging you to give up your beliefs for the sake of a better relationship with your grandchild. I am encouraging more forward thinking. Think through the impact of what you might argue for or against. Then determine whether the argument will deepen your special relationship. You both need a close and loving bond. Will your stance threaten that? If it will, then don't lose your position over an argument that will never be settled peacefully.

I want to be a lifter of burdens for my grandkids, not one who places more on them.

By the time they are teens, they know the difference between right and wrong. They know what scripture has to say about certain issues. Their parents have taught them things they have to sort and figure out for themselves. As a grandparent, I want to help them do that.

It's not my role to fight with them. It's my role to be a sounding board for them. They talk; I listen. I ask if they want input. If they say no, I honor that and stand by them as they figure it out the right way or the hard way. When they make good choices, I rejoice with them. When they make wrong turns, I hurt with them and for them. I don't control their choices or their beliefs. I couldn't even if I argued 'til I'm blue in the face. I have to learn to button it—not agree with it—just hold my opinions until they're invited.

> I want to be a lifter of burdens for my grandkids, not one who places more on them.

That's tough sometimes. I'll admit it. I'm a Texan; a typical Texan who doesn't mind standing for what is right or defending what I believe when challenged. I've even had times when I've encouraged a good fight with a comment like, "Bring it on!" However, I'm careful and wise before I draw a line in the sand and go to battle with my grandkids. I do not want a quick win of a battle that turns into the heartbreaking loss of the war for their love, trust, and special relationship with me.

Grandkids live in a different world today where differing views are prevalent. How they see issues and how we grandparents see them may be as different as night and day. I must keep trying to view it from their perspective if I'm going to have any impact.

Just a couple of days ago I heard from a young lady who is a wonderful friend. However, she wanted to have a conversation with me that had been brewing in her for some time. She wanted to let me know she moved to be with a girl she had fallen in love with. She said, "I'm gay. I love Jesus, and I know that He loves me. I've had to come to terms with that." You know, for some those are fighting words.

Her comments challenged my thinking and beliefs. Because we have developed a trusted relationship over time, I could have asked her any of the following questions. *How can you think that way? What would Jesus say about your comments? How can you justify what the Bible says about homosexuality? Where does this come from? When did all this begin?*

I didn't ask any of those things. I chose to say only, "Sweetheart, I want you to know this. There's nothing you can do to make me love you more, and there's nothing you can do to make me love you less." In a moment I decided the most important way to engage with this dear friend was to communicate a love for our relationship. I let her know I love her dearly. I chose not to correct her. I believe my role is to love. Let the conviction of the Holy Spirit do the correcting. Let the consequences of her choices correct her path. Those life choices, the lifestyle she is embracing, are between her and God.

Saddleback Church Pastor Rick Warren, the author of the best-selling *The Purpose-Driven Life*, once stated,

> Our culture has accepted two huge lies. The first is that if you disagree with someone's lifestyle, you must fear or hate them. The second is that to love someone means you agree with everything they believe or do. Both are nonsense. You don't have to compromise convictions to be compassionate.

Don't compromise your convictions. But make sure your discussions are filled with compassion as you avoid arguments and create an atmosphere of communication that allows for differences of opinion. Those are tough places for your grandkids to find. Jesus said, "Come to me and I will give you rest" (Matthew 11:28). Be like Jesus to your grandkids. Offer them a place of safety and rest, not argument and rejection. If you do, when life gets too tough to handle, they'll run to you.

Chapter 15

Quit Correcting and Start Connecting

Let us think of ways to motivate one another to
acts of love and good works.
Hebrews 10:24 (NLT)

If I spend all my time correcting everything wrong with the kids living with us at Heartlight, I won't have any time left for the relationships God desires for me to have with them. No one can get everything right all the time.

You may see a lot of things wrong with your grandkids. They may get on your last nerves and bring out all your pet peeves. Does any of this sound familiar? They make messes, and we have to clean up after them. Rarely do they help with dishes. They don't sit in chairs correctly. They spend too much time on their phones. They play too many stupid games on the iPads and computers. They lounge around and don't offer to help much with any chores. They don't eat the right things. They park their car in the wrong places. They scrounge around for food, eating my special desserts. They never wash the sheets; much less make the beds before they leave. They track in dirt, clog the drains, leave dirty towels lying around, and run up the electric bill. They dig through my stuff and use whatever they want without asking.

My grandkids' sloppiness may feel like bad manners to me, but do I correct them? Nope. I let it go because I know I need to spend less of our time together correcting and focus my time with them on connecting.

In my seminars for parents of teenagers, I somewhat jokingly tell parents to correct teens only on Mondays, Wednesdays, and Fridays. Give them a break from a culture that is always telling them what they do wrong, how they can do it better, and what they need to do differently next time. I encourage parents to correct, but also to give breaks from correction in the hope that they can create a place of rest for their adolescent children. See, correction may change surface behavior. Connecting changes the heart.

I encourage grandparents not to correct their grandkids at all. Not at all? Am I crazy? I don't think so. Sure, there are things that bug me about my grandkids. However, short of violating the hard-and-fast rules Jan and I have for our home (listed in Chapter 9), we don't correct the grandkids when they visit. Why? Because correction is their parents' job. I believe it's a better strategy for grandparents to give their grandkids a break. Focus on connection with them in ways that build your special relationship. Eventually, they'll do better about their messes because they care about you. (It may take years. Be patient.)

My wife Jan and I have learned to tolerate our grandchildren's inadequacies and sacrifice some of our desires to create an atmosphere where they get a break from the culture they live in every day.

If your coworkers, boss, and customers began to correct you the minute you walked in the door of work every day, you'd quit in a heartbeat. You would not stay long in an atmosphere of constant texts, comments, posts, discussions, and judgments against you. Very few teens survive with their hearts, spirits, and attitudes intact in a world of constant correction.

If your grandson puts in a good day's work mowing your yard, and the first thing you notice is the patch of grass he missed, I guarantee he won't be back to mow again if he can help it. Even if they are true, refrain from comments that his performance wasn't near as good as you hoped, that he mowed it all wrong, or that he didn't quite finish what he started. Those complaints turn his willingness to help into failure. He wasn't good enough. He didn't meet your exacting expectations.

Again, I believe in teaching kids to do a good job. I want kids to experience the benefits of good hard work. But as a grandparent, I don't correct their efforts when they make them. I want them to show up again and keep learning and trying.

If a granddaughter comes over and you don't think she is properly dressed, I'd encourage you to stay away from trying to improve her appearance. Button your lips and don't deliver a message on being modest. If she feels criticized or corrected, she won't be back. You could lose a lifetime of influence in a moment of correction. It's not worth it.

Don't let their behavior get in the way of your special relationship. See the good in them even when it costs you. Speak the language of their heart, not just words to change or stop behaviors. Stop correcting and start connecting.

Understanding their Behavior

I know I've already said this, but it bears repeating. Please don't let your grandkids' displeasing behavior push you away. No matter what they are doing or not doing, love them through it. Even if it feels like what they're doing is breaking your heart, be the one person who sticks by them. I deal with kids who are struggling, and the tendency for parents is to try to manage their child's behavior. In some ways, parents have to do that. Their children are

A wise grandparent will see beyond the behavior and engage in a way that speaks to their hearts.

their responsibility. But behavior management can put a wedge between parents and kids that keep them from getting to the heart of the real issues that are driving the inappropriate actions.

Behavior is goal-oriented. Whatever your grandchild is doing, she is doing it for a reason. There is a method to her madness. There is intention in your grandson's bad behavior. Your grandkids' behavior is a visible expression of the invisible issues within. A wise grandparent will see beyond the behavior and engage in a way that speaks to their hearts. Grandparents should not try to manage grandchildren's actions.

You can help with heart issues by asking questions that help them get to the root of their conduct. If you've done a good job creating a place of rest and a haven of wisdom, grandkids can feel safe sharing what is really going on. This gives you a chance to speak to their deeper internal struggles.

Here are some questions you can ask to get beyond behavior and target the heart:

- Hey, Bud, tell me what's really going on?
- Sweetie, I can see that there's a little bit of conflict. Anything I can help with?
- Tell me what's driving the stuff your parents shared with me?
- Do you think the behavior I see might be connected to something I don't see? What am I not seeing?
- If you could change one thing in your life at the snap of your fingers, what would that be?
- Man, that sounds like a mess. Is there any way I can help in all of this?
- Help me understand what you're thinking. I'm a little confused.
- Hey, how's life in the dark hole? Maybe I can help you find a way out.
- Your words say one thing, but I feel like your behavior says something completely different. Help me identify the difference.

Asking the right question at the right time is an amazing way of opening the door to your grandchild's heart, especially when their answer doesn't invoke a consequence or a form of discipline.

Speaking the Language That Touches their Heart

In 1995, Dr. Gary Chapman wrote a wonderful book called *The Five Love Languages: How to Express Heartfelt Commitment to Your Mate*. This book continues to hit the bestseller lists more than twenty years since it was first published. It's that good. It contains simple truths that are so profound. The book outlines five ways to express and experience love that Chapman calls *love languages*. These five languages are the giving of gifts, quality time, words of affirmation, acts of service, and physical touch.

This book was written for marriages, yet many parents and grandparents have applied the same love language tests to their teens, thinking if they learn how their child (grandchild) receives love, they can better meet their needs.

Not long ago, I was a guest on Gary's *Building Relationships* radio program, a great show produced by Moody Radio. I remember asking him if he thought there were more than five love languages. I don't remember his answer, but it did get me thinking.

Years ago we thought there were just nine planets in our solar system. That's what I learned growing up. That's pretty much the way it was. As young students, we all learned their names by heart and made many mobiles out of coat hangers and Styrofoam balls painted various colors. We made posters and shoebox dioramas of our massive solar system for science projects through my junior high school years.

The great mystery of our time was the planet Pluto that was discovered in 1930. Scientists argued for years over whether it's a planet or not, much like the argument about whether the Beatles' Paul McCartney was indeed the Walrus and possibly died back in the 1970s.

Then something happened in the early 1990s. The first extra-solar planet was discovered, a planet outside of our solar system that orbits a star. What did experts name it? *51 Pegasi B*. It was discovered the same year Gary Chapman's book was published.

Do you want to know how many extra-solar planets have been discovered since that first one? Three thousand, four hundred, and ninety-eight. That's right. We thought there were just nine, and now we know of thirty-five hundred. Amazing, isn't it? The number of planets is far beyond what we could have ever imagined.

I thought if we believed for so long there were just nine planets (Pluto sometimes in, sometimes out), and now there are 3,498, there must be a possibility that when we thought there were just five love languages, there might be a couple more.

I knew there had to be other love languages because those written by Gary never really applied to me. I don't want more gifts because I've got too much stuff already. I don't want quality time because I don't have any more time to give. Words of affirmation feel more like people blowing smoke in my ear (flattery) than real encouragement. I don't want anyone to perform an act of service for me like mowing my grass. I can do that myself or hire someone I trust. Finally, I don't want anyone to touch me. (Do I sound like a crotchety ol' grandpa now?)

> When teens are wronged, they long to have someone rise above the rest and defend them.

Just because those love languages don't fit me doesn't mean they're not true. Of course, they are. I think I'm the odd duck here. How do I feel loved? I spent the next few months thinking about what other love languages might be. Eventually, I came up with a few that touched my heart. I believe these apply to teens everywhere.

Here are two additional ways a grandparent can express love for the adolescent grandchild.

1. *Defend the ones you love. Show your loyalty.* When teens are wronged, they long to have someone rise above the rest and defend them. It affirms a sense of loyalty and commitment to your relationship. It proves you are a high priority in each other's life. A teen desires to know he is loved when all is well. He also wants to know he is loved when things aren't so well, when peers and others turn against him for whatever reason, even if he's wrong. Your grandkids want to know that

when others are against them, you will be for them, speak up for them if need be, and stand by their side. When you listen to them complain about relationships, don't take the other person's side, even if your grandchild is wrong. Over time, most issues will work themselves out and your grandchild will remember how you listened. Show them your loyalty, and they'll feel loved.

2. *An invitation to participate.* Most kids want to be invited to participate, even though they might not attend whatever they've been invited to. I'm the same way. I hate to be left out; just don't expect me to show up when you extend the invitation. I think that I want to be included just as much as teens want to belong. They're desperate to know they are wanted. They want to fit in, long to be popular, desire to be admired. The hardest thing for any teen is to feel left out, excluded, or forgotten about. That's why they're on their phones so much. They don't want to miss anything.

When you defend a grandchild who has been offended, you open the door for a lifelong relationship.

When you invite your grandchildren to join you, you build a relationship.

They will not forget your loyalty or the time you spent with them.

When the Connection Just Isn't Happening

If you're working hard to make a connection and it just doesn't seem to be working, the first thing you must do is ask them some questions.

The first question is this simple one: "What am I doing that is keeping us from connecting?" Flat out ask the question. Send it in a text. Tell your grandchild you'd like to talk about it at some point. Get to the real answer. It may be something you do. It may be something you are saying. They may be embarrassed by your comments. They may think you're goofy. There may be one of your mannerisms that just bug them. It may be how you treat their friends.

Ask the question. Then give them room to answer any way they want. You don't get to defend yourself or question their answer. The issue is not that you are doing something wrong or inappropriate. The focus of the question is to see how you can get past whatever it is that is keeping them from making a connection with you. One of our girls at Heartlight came up to me at one of our family retreats and asked me if I would talk to her grandmother. She said, "Mark, would you talk to my grandmother and tell her and ask her to quit sending me scripture and all her words of encouragement? They make me feel judged, like she just wants to correct me all the time."

The best of intentions can be perceived completely differently.

In this case, a positive, encouraging act done by a grandparent was interpreted as something different by the granddaughter. In time, this young lady will welcome her grandmother's words of encouragement, but for now, she wanted no part of them. The best thing for this grandmother would be to quit texting and wait for a better time to speak in a language her granddaughter could take correctly. The best of intentions can be perceived completely differently. If those good-hearted, intentional acts are getting in the way of a relationship, by all means, stop.

I don't think I've ever read anything about correction being a love language. You can either choose to *correct* their behavior, which is a temporary fix or, you can *connect* for a lifetime.

What do you think your grandchildren really want?

PART IV — YOUR LIFE'S ACTION

Chapter 16

Complaining Ruins Relationships; Gratefulness Draws Them In

When you talk, don't say anything bad. But say the good things
that people need—whatever will help them grow stronger.
Then what you say will be a blessing to those who hear you.
Ephesians 4:29 (ERV)

As the years pass quicker and quicker, we begin to see the unavoidable aging process. We can't help but notice the downward gravitational pull on our bodies. It's inevitable. It's foreseeable. It's certain. We're getting older. The inescapable reality of our fate is that one day we will be gone. What will remain are the memories of who we were. Most won't remember all the things we said, but they will remember how we made them feel. My prayer is that I never make anyone feel uncomfortable around me. So I've made some choices.

Because I don't want to get fat, I work out to make sure I stay in shape the best I can. Because I love good health, I watch what I eat. Because I don't want to break anything, I watch the activities I engage in. Because I don't want two earfuls of hair, age spots all over my face, shriveled and damaged hands, and veins road mapping my nose, I choose dermatological procedures to keep that from happening.

There are choices I can make so my life will be better longer, and there are some things that just aren't under my control.

You know what I want more than anything else? I want to be a grandpa who is grateful for what and who I have in my life. What I don't want to be is a cantankerous old man who is bitter and broken because life didn't turn out the way I planned.

I know this for sure. My wife doesn't want to become a cranky old woman who rants and raves about everything. I can't imagine a Jan who expresses disappointment that life should have treated her better. I know my wife wants to be grateful and thankful for each day God gives her. She is.

These desires go hand-in-hand with the choices we make. Short of developing dementia or losing your physical health, you can choose whether you'll be a cranky ol' woman or that cantankerous ol' man. As long as you have your faculties, you have a choice. That choice determines whether your legacy is a positive one to be remembered or a negative one hopefully quickly forgotten.

I'm not sure people actually realize how they come across. I'm sure most folks prefer to be seen as good-natured. I haven't met anyone who truly wants family, friends, and strangers alike to avoid them. However, many grandparents don't know just how their grandkids see them. I interviewed a number of teens and asked them to tell me about their grandparents. Some of their answers were not complimentary. Most were just sad. Here's how they described some of their grandparents:

- Very bitter about everything.
- Full of disappointment.
- Argues about everything, is just looking for a fight.
- Has become crabby and disagreeable.
- Judgmental attitude toward everything.
- Opinionated, with outbursts full of gripes or criticisms.
- Complains about everything.
- Unreasonable, belligerent, and grouchy.
- Never shuts up.

With some degree of certainty, I'm pretty sure I've never met a grandparent who said, "You know, I sure would like to be like…" any one of the statements I just listed. But it happens. When grandparents wonder why their grandkids don't want to be in their presence, it baffles me how many don't have a clue why they are being avoided.

Let me ask you something. Would you really like to hang around someone who displays any of the characteristics on that list? I wouldn't. While I say that, I'm scared to death I might unknowingly be like, or become like the things on that list.

Here are a couple of things you can do to find out if you have become an offensive person who is to be avoided. Ask God to search your heart. Psalm 139:23-24 says,

> Search me, God, and know my heart; test me and know my anxious thoughts. See if there is any offensive way in me, and lead me in the way everlasting.

You can pray for God to reveal what it is in you pushing your grandchildren away. It may be the very thing your spouse has said for years. You probably heard it from your kids when they lived in your home. Perhaps co-workers or bosses said it to you or about you.

I'm sure you know there's some truth in the harder words that have come your way through various people all your life. Your relationships and your legacy hang in the balance here. It's time to deal with those unpleasant ways you've developed, so you can ensure your legacy is one to be remembered, not one to be quickly forgotten.

Ask your grandkids. If you're afraid to ask your kids and grandkids how they see you, that's a good indicator you might have some areas to work on. Text them and try it. Pure and simple, you know kids will say things in texts they wouldn't say face-to-face. So ask them. Text them these questions, "What is that makes you want to avoid me? What am I doing to push you away, because that's not what I want to do?"

If they text back, "You complain and gripe about everything," don't rush to explain, excuse, or justify. Accept their words, tell them thanks for sharing, and begin to change. Even at your age, you can make new habits, especially if the old ones are getting between you and your grandkids.

No one likes a complainer or grumbler, one who is discontent with his lot in life. Remember Philippians 2:14?

Do everything without complaining and arguing.

Most teens avoid constant complainers, including grandparents, like the plague. They live in this culture of negativity all the time. If that's what they're going to get from grandma and grandpa too, they will look elsewhere for their encouragement and assurance of hope. There isn't any hope to be found in one who complains all the time.

I've met many people aging with a great deal of anger, unhappy that life didn't turn out the way they hoped, critical of folks and God because they feel abandoned. If life is now a half-empty glass, these folks look at the empty portion all the time. They focus all their remaining energies on their losses and disappointments. These are reflected in their words, actions, and constant rants about how life would have been different if they were dealt a different set of cards to play. Their words already speak death, not a grateful heart and a hope of heaven to come.

I recently talked to a friend I've known for forty years. He began to speak of an incident that happened to him thirty-eight years ago. His discussion centered on how his life would have been so different if the pastor of the church he worked for almost four decades before had treated him differently. The discussion wasn't just a few sentences of disgust or disappointment. It lasted for forty-five minutes! This friend spent thirty-eight years rolling the scenario of disappointment around in his head, justifying his own loss, blaming someone else, and expressing his disappointment in life through his words and comments.

Disappointment in life comes out as anger. Anger and unforgiveness dig roots of bitterness and resentment, which foster arguments, fighting, crabbiness, judgmental tendencies, disagreeableness, opinionated harping, as well as complaining, griping, and being grouchy and unreasonable. Anger and unforgiveness never offer hope.

There are some battlefields where wars continue to be fought, even though the enemy is long gone. Those are the battlefields of your mind and your emotions. If you find yourself stuck, it will pour out on those around you. If you know there are things from the past you can't get past, it's time to get some help in the form of counseling and therapy. Even at your age, it is well worth

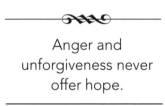

Anger and unforgiveness never offer hope.

the time and effort to become healthy. Then you can be a testimony of forgiveness, an example of healing and wholeness, and a beacon of hope to your grandchildren. I do believe you can teach an old dog new tricks. It's never too late to mend fences, and one is never too old to change his ways.

Gratefulness

Remember earlier in the book when I mentioned that one of the jobs of a grandparent is to give perspective? Here's a hopeful story I offer to anyone who experienced disappointment and loss in their life.

I had high expectations for a particular fellow in my life. As the years passed, I found I grew angrier and angrier with him. I expected him to be something he never was. I wanted him to give me things he never gave. Every time I saw him I thought about how he hurt and upset me by failing to meet my expectations and give me opportunities to forge a deeper relationship with him.

I was angry for years—that quiet kind of anger that simmers continuously but never really spews over to anyone else. I just felt a sting whenever I thought about this person. Ever had anger like that?

Then I had a dream. I dreamed I died and went to heaven. As I approached God, I noticed this person, the object of my years of anger, was standing next to Him as I was ushered into His presence. My anger boiled over. I was mad that this person was standing next to God after continually disappointing me. I expressed my feelings to God, using some words I was shocked I would say to Him even in a dream.

God quickly stopped me. He answered with a short remark that changed my life. He said, "Mark, I want you to know something. I've been using this person in your life to mold you into the person I wanted you to be." You know, that's all I needed to hear to understand why that happened in my life. Since that dream, I have felt no anger towards this person at all.

What I thought was so bad was really a good thing. It's all about perspective. Because of my God-given new perspective, I'm not angry. Instead, I became extremely grateful for my circumstances. It's just sad that it took me until I was in my fifties before I realized what He was doing.

A heart full of gratefulness leaves no room for complaining. There's just something about a thankful person that is attractive and appealing.

It's as simple as this. Every time I cook a meal at our home when my granddaughter Macie comes over to eat, she always—I mean always—says, "Thanks for dinner, Poppa." That is a simple comment, but it moves me every time. Her gratitude expressed in just those four words makes me want to cook every meal for her and make it the best it can be.

> A heart full of gratefulness leaves no room for complaining.

I know what I don't want to become in my older years. Ungrateful. I know exactly what I want for my grandchildren as they grow older—hope and gratefulness. I want them to be chock-full of hope and crammed with gratefulness for the life before them. I want them to know that whatever they face, they can get through it. If you complain and are ungrateful for where you are in life, it speaks volumes to teens that feel like they sometimes can't make it through the next week.

Regardless of your current circumstances, if you are grateful for who you are, what you have, and whom you have in your life, that's a legacy that will be talked about long after you're gone.

When you have hope, your grandchildren start to believe they can make it too. When they are overwhelmed, your joy and grateful heart can restore and refuel them. Because of what they see and hear from you, they believe they can move past tough situations. It also puts life into better perspective for teens; it tells them their hard days will pass. They will mess up, blow it, and let people down. Other people they count on will mess up, blow it, and let them down. Still, hope can prevail because they have seen you get through similar or worse situations.

> Weeping may last through the night, but joy comes with the morning. (Psalm 30:5, NLT)

My dear friend Chelsea Cameron has been a guest on our radio show for years. Her words are impactful, and her message touches hearts as she shares her views on parenting. The most profound comment I've heard from her is the message she wants to communicate to her kids. "On our best of days, and our worst of days, I want you to know that our family is better because you are in it." Wow! What a message to convey to a tired and weary teen searching for significance and security. What hope to offer a kid who longs to belong to a family that will never quit on him!

Okay, Grandparents, now you have a choice. Do you want to be a cantankerous ol' man or cranky ol' woman? Or would you rather be grandparents full of hope, ones who are grateful for God's presence in their lives?

It's your choice. Choose wisely, my friends.

Chapter 17

Can Everyone Just Laugh a Little?

A cheerful heart is good medicine,
but a crushed spirit dries up the bones.
Proverbs 17:22

When we started our *Parenting Today's Teens* radio program ten years ago, we traveled the country peddling our program to radio stations everywhere. We hoped they would pick it up and give us a chance to prove that parents and grandparents were searching for help and hope in raising teens. We relentlessly pursued these stations. Radio programmers did not want to take a chance. They had no idea who I was.

To them, I came out of left field, starting a radio broadcast at age fifty-two. I had no previous history of recording or even an understanding of how to get people to carry our program. When this guy in jeans and boots, with a mustache from the nineteenth century, strolled into radio stations, programmers had not seen anything like it before. Add the fact that I wanted to do a program about dealing with teens, and that was a curveball for most.

Nevertheless, some gave us a chance. Now many stations air our program, and it does well. We are thrilled to partner with so many wonderful radio stations throughout North America.

One organization asked if they could test the waters first. They wanted to see how I do while *on mic* (live on the air). They invited me to come in and do a drive-time program on a Tuesday morning from six to eight o'clock. The first hour would be me talking with the morning show host. The second hour would be me answering calls from the listening audience. Our radio team thought this would be a great opportunity to show who we were and give the radio station and their audience a taste of what we were all about. We decided to go, in hopes of them carrying our program.

Well, the day before I was to go on-air with this station, a national scandal broke about a pastor. This pastor, who had been very anti-homosexual in his preaching and critical of the gay lifestyle, had made headlines once before when he got caught in a homosexual relationship exposed by his partner. Now, this pastor was in the national news again. The new story proclaimed the pastor one hundred percent heterosexual after going through counseling. Many news sources covered the story.

It was a big story when he was exposed; it was now bigger news that he had been restored in his relationship with his family. Again, this story broke the day before my trial run on this radio group, a group that was pretty conservative. Okay, it was very conservative.

Anyway, we got to the studio early the next day; and our radio producer and good friend Roger looked at me and said, "Okay, Mark, now don't blow it!" The radio station's people all gathered to watch the guy with the mustache and to make a determination about carrying our program. I was on one side of the glass booth with the morning show host. Everyone else was on the other side observing while sipping coffee.

The show began. For the first hour, I answered questions, had a great conversation about teens, and discussed the needs of adolescents. I told parents how they could counter the effects this contrary culture was having on their family. Everyone on the other side of the glass smiled, loved the interaction, and gave winks or nods at key moments to let me know of their approval.

Then the second hour began. The host opened up the phone lines to take a few questions from the listening audience. Guess what the first question was? It was a young lady who said, "Mark, I have a question for you. Are you one hundred percent heterosexual?"

The folks on the other side of the glass slowly lowered their coffee cups in anticipation of my answer. Our producer Roger crossed his arms, then held his head in his hands. He rubbed his forehead and didn't even look up.

I answered, "You know, I don't think so." One would have thought I just stated the Pope isn't Catholic. Birds quit chirping, all traffic stopped, and the radio folks gasped when I made this comment.

"You know, I don't think so," I repeated. "I think I'm ninety-five percent heterosexual, three percent metrosexual because I wear Tommy Bahama shirts occasionally, and two percent homosexual because I'd kiss Keith Urban if I had a chance." (Keith Urban is a country singer married to actress Nicole Kidman. I've been a fan for years.) I thought it was the perfect answer. Behind the smile on my face, I was belly laughing, thinking I just hit it out of the park with such a humorous response. The radio guys did not agree.

Immediately, the live show switched to the weatherman sharing the forecast for the day. The next sound I heard was a loud rapping on the window and the producer saying, "You can't say that! YOU CAN'T SAY THAT!" Everybody got very quiet. All you could hear was the weather report droning on in the background. I thought this was a great defining moment for me to let them know who I am.

I stood up, looked through the glass at all the radio execs, and simply stated, arms stretched out, "If you guys don't lighten up, you'll never be able to discuss the hard issues with teens or their parents."

Great story, eh? Okay, I embellished a little, but you get my point. Right? You've got to lighten up. So many take everything so seriously that their intended message isn't accepted because of the sourpuss look on the messenger's face.

I was speaking in Duck Dynasty Land last year and told this radio story to a church congregation. They roared with laughter. A seventy-five-year-old lady came up to thank me for my comments afterward. She said, "We haven't laughed like that in this church for twenty-five years!"

Then a thirty-year-old guy came up and said, "Mark, you know you can throw a bigger brick if it's wrapped in humor." Here was a young man who got it. My sentiments exactly.

Here are a couple of quotes from one of my heroes who evidently thinks like I do:

> If you're not enjoying most of your day, if you've stopped having fun, you're missing more than you are contributing. (Swindoll, 2015)

> How is your sense of humor? Are the times in which we live beginning to be reflected in your attitude, your face, and your outlook? Solomon says three things will occur when we have lost our sense of humor: a broken spirit, a lack of inner healing, and dried-up bones (Proverbs 15:13, 15; 17:22). What a barren portrait! Humor is not a sin. It is a God-given escape hatch; a safety valve. Being able to see the lighter side of life is a rare, vital virtue. (Swindoll, 220)

I'm not encouraging laughing everything off. Nor am I suggesting you make a joke of everything. Good jokes do not make bad things good. Proverbs 25:10 (NLT) states,

> Singing cheerful songs to a person with a heavy heart is like taking someone's coat in cold weather or pouring vinegar in a wound.

You have to be careful how you use humor but lightening a heavy moment with humor can make a hard truth easier to digest.

I encourage grandparents to lighten up a bit. Don't make everything so serious in your approach to your grandkids. You can talk about some very, very serious issues and still laugh in the middle of those hard discussions. Laughter lets them know your relationship is still intact, no matter how hard the conversation is. Hope is instilled, no matter how tough the situation, because you can still smile. Don't minimize the situation, but don't make it any bigger and heavier than it has to be.

Laughter is a form of worship. It lets everyone hear the confidence you have that God is still in control in the midst of whatever is happening. Your wisdom can be received and perhaps better acknowledged when you don't have a frown on your face.

After living with thousands of teens, I know laughter is greatly needed in kids' lives. Their lives are so heavy. Their poor choices and consequences are sometimes grim. Life has gotten so hard. They need to learn again how to have some innocent fun. There's nothing funny or humorous when a teen is struggling. Truly, there's nothing funny about kids who have given up hope. But there is a need for fun and laughter to instill a new sense of hope.

Don't minimize the situation, but don't make it any bigger and heavier than it has to be.

When I finally hear laughter from a struggling teen, I know they are on a path to healing. Learning to laugh again becomes an essential part of discovering a renewed sense of hope.

Look for the Humor in Situations

Some of the greatest comedians spend their lives helping us look and laugh at ourselves. It's healthy. We're funny people. Just spend a little time at the mall or an airport, and you'll laugh when you see what a funny-looking and weird-acting species we are. When you laugh, remember people are laughing at you as much as you are laughing at them!

Do you think Jesus and the disciples ever had a good laugh? I mean, a hold-your-belly-crying-tears-can't-get-your-breath laugh that just couldn't stay contained? I think so. Here was a carpenter, a handful of fishermen, a tax collector, and the Lord only knows what everyone else did as an occupation (That's a joke!), and you don't think they laughed and told jokes?

Some of my funniest times in life have been when I'm with other fishermen. We tell stories, joke with one another, and have all kinds of fun catching our next meal. I bet you Jesus and the disciples were even told to keep it down a bit when they visited restaurants and stayed at inns.

There is a time for everything, including laughter.

A time to weep and a time to laugh, a time to mourn and a time to dance. (Ecclesiastes 3:4)

Look for Opportunities to Have a Good Belly Laugh

I recently had dinner with a family. They asked me to come by and spend the evening observing them. The parents wanted ideas to help change the declining relational atmosphere within their home. After an entire evening with the parents and three kids (two were teens), I asked the mom why it was so quiet around the table at dinner. Her response shocked me. She said, "We don't allow any laughter at the dinner table."

My comment shocked her. "You've got to be kidding me! That's horrible!" I said.

I never heard anyone come right out and say that. However, I've seen it implied in many different grandparents' homes. They're the ones where grandkids would choose to be elsewhere if they could.

I never limit laughter in my home. When my grandkids visit, I believe it's more important for them to have fun than to sit down and listen to my teaching, lessons, and diatribes about leading a successful and fruitful life. Why? Because if we have some fun and learn to laugh, the doors of their hearts will swing open. Their ears will open to hear what I need to share in the days ahead.

Here are some ways to add fun to your home:

- Watch a funny movie (one *they* think is funny).
- Grab an iPad and try to beat each other in a contest to find the funniest comedian on YouTube.

- Hold a joke night at dinner where everyone has to come to the table with a joke ready to be told. (Then give a prize of twenty dollars for the best joke.)
- Sit around the fireplace and tell the funniest stories you've ever heard.
- Spend time jokingly commenting on past events. Laugh about people's responses.

I like this quote:

I have not seen anyone dying of laughter, but I know millions who are dying because they are not laughing. (Kataria, 2010 Tweet)

Tell a Few Jokes and Give Yourself Permission to Laugh

One of the most serious men I've ever met makes sure he tells no less than three jokes when you are in his presence. It's become his trademark. And he tells the best jokes. Really. No one has an excuse for not being able to find good jokes for any age, as there are millions on the Internet. Why not greet your grandkids

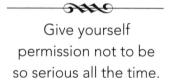

Give yourself permission not to be so serious all the time.

at the door with a joke, saying, "Here, I got a good one for you!"

Give yourself permission not to be so serious all the time. Lighten up a little. Exaggerate your stories a bit to get a good response. Tell a joke to add some humor. Make fun of yourself, so your grandkids know you can have fun as much as the next guy. Laugh at your own mistakes so your grandkids will know you'll laugh at some of theirs.

Laughter is something that comes from within, reflecting an inner peace and the humility to let go and have a good chuckle.

Hey, put a smile back on your face. It's contagious.

Chapter 18

You're Kidding Me.
This is Important?

So we fix our eyes not on what is seen, but on what is unseen,
since what is seen is temporary, but what is unseen is eternal.
2 Corinthians 4:18

Jan and I found a place of rest in a little town called San José del Cabo, located on the peninsula of Baja, California. We retreat there quite a bit to rest, write, and take a break from my crazy travel schedule.

Last August we left our home to go to our little airport in Longview, Texas, on our way to San José del Cabo. We reached the airport at 4:30 p.m. and pulled my truck up to the front door to unload our bags. It's a tiny airport with only one gate to depart and arrive; and only two flights a day. I jumped out of the car to help unload our bags and ran in to get us all checked in.

In the process of checking in, a couple of Jan's bags were overweight. That was no surprise to me, as the way Jan packs her belongings looks more like we're moving to Mexico than just visiting for a week. It took us twenty minutes to get it all straightened out, making sure we were within weight limits. The baggage was then sent off to be loaded onto the plane. The flight was already boarding, so we hurried through security, got on the plane, and flew to Dallas to await our next flight.

When we got to Dallas, we were told the next leg of our trip was delayed for four hours because of weather. We ate dinner, walked around a bit, and sat and waited to board the plane for our retreat to Mexico. As we finally got on the plane at midnight, now eight hours after we arrived at the Longview airport, I remembered something. The minute I stepped on the plane, I looked at Jan and said, "I left the truck running out in front of the airport in Longview." I never went back outside and parked it! I couldn't believe it.

The flight attendant next to me heard my comment and decided to announce it to the whole plane. Everyone laughed at my forgetfulness. I quickly sat down and got on my phone amidst the chuckles and comments. I quickly called my daughter, hoping she could run to the airport and get my truck.

"Hey, Melissa, sorry to wake you up," I said.

"Are you guys in Mexico yet?" She replied.

"No, we were delayed a bit and just now got on the plane out of Dallas. I called because I need you to do something. I need you to go to the airport and get my truck."

I could tell she wasn't real excited about getting out of bed at midnight to help me when she said, "Sure, but why?"

"Your *mom* left the truck running in front of the airport," I replied. "Okay, I did it. But if Jan's bags hadn't been overweight, I would have remembered to go park it. So really it was her fault, right?"

What is the moral of my story? Many times, in pursuit of what we think is *important* (of great significance), we forget about that which is most *valuable* (of considerable importance and great worth).

For the sake of this chapter, let me clarify that what is *important* is usually focused on the here and now, and what is *valuable* has to do with that which will retain future value.

There are many things you wake up to each day that you think are important to complete or finish. Those important and much-needed tasks to complete nag at you until they are finished. They have an amazing way of eating up time, energy, and resources. The same time, energy, and resources could be expended to complete things that are more valuable and longer lasting.

Call it the tyranny of the urgent or exchanging what is valuable for that which is urgent. Important things may be easier or screaming to be handled quickly. The reality is that many important matters take away opportunities for some pretty valuable intentions.

You may think it important to play golf, mow the yard, or spend the weekend working around the house, but what may be more valuable is hanging out with a granddaughter who just broke up with a boyfriend. That golf course will always be there, and that grass will always keep growing, but your granddaughter will one day move away.

You may think it important to do your own thing, but what may be more valuable is being with your grandson and creating some memories. Your stuff can wait, but your grandson won't be around long.

You may think it important to go fishing with your buddies, but what may be more valuable is taking a grandchild fishing so you all can spend some time together. Your time with your grandchild can change his life, and it's doubtful your buddy's life will change much because you hung out on a boat.

You may think it important to go on a mission trip on the other side of the world to visit orphans, but what may be more valuable is spending time with a granddaughter who has been bullied and beaten up by some friends. You can go on a mission trip later. You won't always be able to comfort a hurt little girl who calls you Poppa.

You may think it important to do something for others, but what may be more valuable is to do something for your family who hasn't seen you in a while. Others can wait; your family won't.

You may think it important to buy that new flat-panel TV, golf club, gun, or tool for your garage; but it may be more valuable to invest that money in purchasing something for your grandson, something he will remember forever.

You may think it important to host a dinner for friends, but what may be more valuable is to spend time with a granddaughter who doesn't feel like she has any friends. There's always another meal to eat with your peers, but never another opportunity like this.

You may think it important to complete your project, but it may be more valuable to get that ice cream with a grandson or granddaughter who just needs some hang time with Grandma or Grandpa.

Maybe baking those cookies with a granddaughter is the very thing that saves her life...*seriously*! If you don't think so, then you don't understand the power you possess as a grandparent to bring hope to any situation.

What is the most valuable thing you can do for a grandchild? Invest your time. Invest your money. Invest your heart. That's what it will cost you. It's a big price, but the rewards for your involvement will return to you a hundred-fold in the way your family views you now and how they will remember you later.

Here's what I think is valuable in the lives of your grandchildren and worthy of your provision:

A Listening Ear

Everyone needs a valued listener, and your grandkids are no exception. Think about it. Who do they have that will really sit down, listen, and give them a place to vent and spew, complain, and criticize?

A young lady made a hurtful comment to me last week. She got in trouble for being disrespectful to some of our Heartlight staff. I merely said, "Want to hear some advice to get out of this mess?" I thought she would say, "Sure!" or "Yes, please tell me what I need to do." or "I would love to hear what you have to say." Those weren't her comments. She said, "Why would I listen to you? You don't even know who I am!"

> Listening includes a heartfelt desire to get to know the person you're listening to.

She was teaching me once again a lesson I've heard many, many times before. You can't just listen for the sake of listening. Listening includes a heartfelt desire to get to know the person you're listening to or they will smell a rat a mile away. Grandkids know when you have an interest in their lives and want to hear all about them, and when you're just listening because that's what a good grandparent is supposed to do.

They want someone to listen to them. And they want to be heard by someone who has an interest in them. You can be that person. That's more than important. It's more than valuable. That's invaluable.

Access to Wise Counsel

Sometimes grandkids need to vent to let out their frustrations. They must vent to someone who will keep private their stupid comments and absurd accusations. They know they're being ridiculous. They're just mad, and they want to get that anger out. You can be a safe place where they can let off some of their steam, without scolding or making fun of what they say.

Now, if a grandchild's comments are a violation of parents' rules or reflect a potentially damaging situation, then you need to share their rant with their parents. Make sure your grandchild knows that's the action you're going to take. But for the most part, a listening ear is all that is needed to calm your teen grandkids down when life throws them a curveball. After their tongues rattle a while, their minds usually kick back in gear and they come to some better conclusions than where they started.

Give them time to speak what is on their hearts or stuck in their heads, and they'll either come to some resolution or ask you a question to help them get to one. When you have been this funnel of frustration a number of times, you'll begin to win the right to be heard in the deeper, harder issues your grandchild will eventually bring to the table. I call those *decision-discussions* where they genuinely want to know what you think so they can come to a decision about something on their hearts.

Typical teens learn from their own experiences. Wise teens learn from the experiences of others. Teens can't become wise if they don't have those others they can trust. Grandparents are in the perfect position to help their teens gain wisdom from their experiences. The grandparent with the listening ear can move a grandchild to a deeper level where they know there is always available understanding, compassionate listening, and healthy processing of their emotional turmoil. That's more than important or valuable. It's absolutely invaluable.

Affirmation of Who They Are

The way you listen probably sends a greater message of hope than any words out of your mouth. Just as you know when someone is preoccupied with some other matter when you are talking, your grandchild knows the same. Any hint of distraction or disinterest will force your grandchild to search for another empathetic listening ear. Make sure you give your undivided attention when you sit and listen.

> The way you listen probably sends a greater message of hope than any words out of your mouth.

Pick a place conducive to listening. Create an atmosphere where you won't be interrupted.

I usually pick a restaurant I know will be quiet. My grandkids know that when I want to sit down and talk with them, we're going to a quiet place and we're going to sit in the back where interruptions are minimal. I plan it that way, and they expect it. I want them to know they are the most important things in my life when I sit down and open my ears to their hearts.

If you're like most granddads, you want to fix any problem they talk about. If you're like most grandmoms, you might want to give ten answers to their problem with personal scenarios for each. Many times, all grandchildren need is someone to listen. I would encourage you not to try to fix or solve their issues. Just convey hope and tell them how special they are. Remind them of who they are whenever they forget.

You don't have to have an eloquent array of words. Just make them feel they are just as important to you now, sitting across from you in a discussion, as they were the day you first held them in your arms. Assure them they continue to be a blessing to your family, as they were the day they came into this world. Help them remember those who love them, rely on them, and with whom they have some very special and exceptional relationships. Make your teen grandkids feel valued. This is more than valuable—it's invaluable.

A Refuge from the Storms of Life

Like I stated earlier, grandparents can provide a safe place during the storms of their teen grandkids' lives. When they are battered by the culture, swing wide the doors of your home and your hearts. See the preciousness in the most messed-up, beat-up grandchild of yours. You create an atmosphere of hope and refuge when you listen and accept them right where they are.

Teenage grandkids don't come to see you just because you're their grandparent. They come to you because of what they see in you and how you respond to them in various situations. They come to you because of how they see you treat others. They come because they've heard your compassion, seen your heart, and felt your kindness. They watch and learn even at times when they are not asking you to listen. Based on what they see in you, they will determine how much of a refuge you can be.

The life message to be transferred here is that they can find rest in your presence. With you, they can take a break from the normal busyness of life, and they can find a place of comfort when the storms of life are raging. That's more than valuable—it's invaluable.

Transitioning from Theoretical Truth to Practical Application

One of the most valuable roles a grandparent plays in the lives of their grandchildren is helping them take the theoretical truths they have learned through their formative years and apply them in practical ways. This can be one of the most challenging, but rewarding, aspects of grandparenting. When they participate in this awakening, Grandma and Grandpa get to have an amazing impact on the hearts of their grandkids.

Here's an example. Most grandkids have heard Romans 8:28, "And we know that in all things God works for the good of those who love him, who have been called according to his purpose." They've heard it a million times, right? In one sense, it is theoretical truth for them until there comes a time for practical application.

That happens with a loss or a quick turn of events that changes the direction of a family. It might be a disaster, a catastrophe, or a hard-to-understand act of violence. It might even be a personal failure. In these situations, grandchildren need the wisdom of their grandparents to help them understand and comprehend what that particular scripture really means.

This transition of truth to an application isn't just accepted. It is transferred. It's something valuable that can only be done by a select few in a family. It's helping them balance what they know to be true with the way they feel. That's even more than valuable—it's invaluable.

The Bigger-Picture Perspective

I've mentioned this earlier but can't reiterate enough how valuable your perspective on life can be to your grandchildren. How many of your grandkids have a trusted someone who is older, more experienced, wiser, and as available as you are as their grandparent—especially someone within the context of family tradition, generational habits, and connected relationships? There aren't many. Besides, it's your job.

Grandparents are the ones to bring hope to the table, looking beyond what is seen, and having faith because of their experiences in the past. Grandparents offer the bigger-picture perspective. That's invaluable.

Help with the Puzzle of Life

Ever put together one of those thousand-piece puzzles you spread out over a table, and all gather around doing their part? It's funny to me that these usually take place at family events. The process pretty much reflects God's piecing together of His masterpiece through all the family members putting together their conglomeration of jagged parts.

Usually, people put together the borders first, kind of the outline of the work of art to come. The border holds the puzzle pieces together as they are joined and connected to create a beautiful picture.

Everyone usually selects a part of the puzzle and begins their work. They search and try to make the pieces fit, just like in life. I don't know about you, but usually, during this table activity, I hear the following comments from my grandkids:

- This piece doesn't fit.
- There are some pieces missing.
- I don't get how this is going to look.
- These just don't go together.
- I'm getting worn out.
- This is taking so much time.

Wise grandparents keep folks (grandkids and all) on course by responding with the following:

- This is how it fits together.
- Take your time; there's no hurry.
- Let's look at the bigger picture.
- Each piece is important.
- The dark pieces are just as needed as the brighter pieces.
- Keep going. It's coming together.

Throughout the process, wise grandparents explain how it takes all colors to bring about the majesty of this masterpiece (just like life). How it takes time to get things right (just like life). How the dark pieces make the brighter pieces come to life (just like life). See my point? Helping grandkids put together a jigsaw puzzle is a lot like helping them put together the pieces of their lives. When you help them see and understand the similarities? That's invaluable.

Wise grandparents sacrifice the important things of today for the more valuable stuff of the future. That's what they do best. Oh, and about my truck? Yes, it ran for eight hours at the airport that night. The door was partway open and the radio playing. That's how small our airport is.

Fortunately for me, my focus on the important didn't cost me what was more valuable. Putting your focus on your awesome grandkids? That's invaluable.

Chapter 19

Won't Somebody Just Listen!

Do nothing out of selfish ambition or vain conceit. Rather, in
humility value others above yourselves, not looking to your
own interests but each of you to the interests of the others.
Philippians 2:3-4

If there is ever a time that adolescents are looking for someone to listen, it is now. Over the last few years, I've watched our culture move away from some very basic principles and values necessary for relational interaction to an atmosphere where communication is more about the one-way expression of one's thoughts and beliefs than the two-way street of someone actively listening to the hearts of people struggling to be heard.

Throughout this book, I emphasize again and again how vital it is for grandparents to listen and actively show concern for the viewpoints of others. Effective communication and discussion depend on focusing on others more than yourself.

Let me use an example of a well-known group called Black Lives Matter, an organization formed in 2012. It is working to validate black lives. The slogan "Black Lives Matter" hit the news media a few years ago, and the immediate response was "All Lives Matter" from many across the country. This slogan became a springboard for other various slogans like "Blue Lives Matter," "Gay Lives Matter," and "Firefighters' Lives Matter." The focus of public response was shifted to other groups who tried to invalidate the Black Lives Matter message by stating that others' lives matter just as much. In other words, people jumped to express their own beliefs, to override or ignore the initial message of Black Lives Matter.

Now, don't think this is a political statement. Please don't take my comments as a justification for anyone, and don't focus on the purpose and mission of any of these groups. I'm just pointing out the responses to this organization. I hardly know what any of the groups mentioned above believe or promote. It's just that I thought it odd that one group wanted to be heard and shared their concern, and many chose to respond with their own favorite slogan rather than listen. Many missed the original message the Black Lives Matter group was trying to communicate. In terms of true communication, the public's response was about as legitimate and effective as the following two examples:

My wife tearfully came to me years ago and in so many words said, "Mark, I was sexually abused for a number of years." If my response had been insensitive, "Well, Jan, there were a lot of people that were sexually abused," I'm sure it would have significantly affected our relationship and marriage. Her message would have been missed, her heart not heard because of my insensitivity and my need to respond rather than listen.

What if my grandchild came to me and shared that he was getting bullied at school and had been beaten up a few times, and my response was, "Well, a lot of people are bullied and beaten up at school?" I'm again sure this kind of response would shut down our relationship and probably preclude any future communication. The request for help and reaching out for hope was ignored, and the heart hardened by the hard-hearted response.

When people aren't heard, they start to scream the message louder. When that louder message isn't heard, then they become activists, actively behaving in a way to get other people's attention. Can you relate the same type of behavior to struggling teens? How about struggling grandchildren?

I wonder if unruly grandchildren would have reached the point of acting out if their grandparents had actively listened. If grandparents listen to a teen grandchild in the initial stages of her problems, isn't that likely to help before she gets hurt? I guarantee that a teen not paid attention to will eventually get your attention one way or another.

The key to active listening is to understand what you hear. Be aware of your filters. Our filters interpret and translate how we hear the message coming from our grandchild. Our filters might include how we were raised, our traditions, our hurts, our perceptions, our background, our own beliefs and our values. Our own trust issues, our age, and our experiences can taint the messages we hear.

The challenge is to remove our filters and listen through our grandchildren's grid. We need to understand where they are coming from, not filter what they're saying

> The key to active listening is to understand what you hear.

through where we've been. If we hear it how they're saying it, then we'll be connecting.

Make it your goal to understand your grandchildren's world and filter their message in the way that looks out for their interest, not your own. Effective grandparents are good listeners who possess the ability to look to the interests of their grandchildren in the grandchildren's world and not lean on their own understanding of their own world. That's called participatory listening.

As I've said before, many grandparents get so intent on sharing their message that they forget about hearing the message from their grandchild. Your interaction with your grandchild has got to be about them, not about you. A good listener has the ability to let people know they matter without saying a word. Good listeners have the amazing ability to speak to the heart because they understand where the heart of their grandchildren is.

Let's repeat some of the most infamous conversation stoppers and offer some practical ways to improve your listening skills with your grandchildren.

Invite Them Over

How you respond to your grandchildren early in life will determine how they respond to you later in life. Isn't it ironic how annoyed we can get when our younger grandkids always want something, ask for everything, and never quit talking? Then they enter their teen years, and we wish they would tell us what they want, ask us questions, and maintain discussions with us?

Let your teen grandkids know you are still there for them. The welcome mat is always out to discuss anything. They can come on over anytime. When you're sitting around the dinner table when they visit, instead of always wanting to share your opinion, let them know you would love to hear what they have to say. When they speak, make sure you give them eye contact to let them know you are listening.

Listen Now. Don't Wait.

Timing is everything. If the opportunity to listen arises, make it a priority. When grandchildren want to talk, don't put them off or let it go until the weekend. If they have something on their hearts, then give them the opportunity to share it with you as soon as possible. Putting them off only sends the message that they just aren't important right now. If you find yourself always saying, "Let's talk later," you're missing some connecting opportunities.

Understand, Not Necessarily Agree

Chances are you are anywhere from forty-five to seventy years older than your grandchildren. That is a huge age difference. So expect that there will be huge differences in the way your grandchildren perceive relationships and newsworthy events. Call it a generation gap, if you will. There are just differences—differences that will come up in your discussions.

Do this at the onset of a discussion: Let them know it is okay not to agree on everything. It's essential that the goal of your discussions is to bring you guys to understanding, not necessarily agreement.

When my grandkids want to have a discussion about a serious topic, whether it be abortion, marijuana, terrorism, war, or politics, I say this to them first. "I know that we won't agree on everything, but by helping me understand how you think, you may move me closer to appreciating your viewpoint."

This comment diffuses any potential argument. Comments like this let your grandchildren know you don't want to argue. You want to discuss. Discussion stoppers and *fighting words* include, but are certainly not limited to, the following:

- Where did that come from?
- Who told you that?
- Are you kidding me?
- That's stupid.
- Did you come up with that on your own?
- That's hard to believe!
- That's wrong.

Some comments that help your conversation move forward positively are more along the lines of these:

- That's interesting.
- Wow, that's different.
- I never thought of that.
- Hmmmmm…
- I see where you're coming from.
- I've never heard it said that way before.

Hey, when I'm having a discussion with a grandchild, or any kid for that matter, I want to do all I can to ensure the conversation is engaging and will be one we can continue in the future. Don't you?

Don't Interrupt. It's a No-No

When you interrupt mid-sentence, interject a thought, or just blurt out what you're thinking and don't let your grandchildren complete their comments, you tell them you aren't listening. You're not valuing them. You're devaluing them.

Let them finish their sentences and comments. Don't stop their flow of words. You worked hard to get this fire going. Don't put it out with interruptions that douse any chance you'll have for further conversations.

If you're both interrupters, then set up a plan and say, "Hey, you speak a paragraph, and then let me speak a paragraph. I want to hear all you're saying and don't want to interrupt." One practical tool for interrupters is to pass an object back and forth. Give your grandchildren a penny, a rock, a dollar or whatever object you choose. Tell them you won't speak or respond to what they're saying until they pass you the chosen object. When you have the object, they can't speak. This can help you break the bad habit of interrupting.

Don't Correct During Conversations

Ever been in conversations where there's so much correction going on you forget what the subject of the conversation was in the first place? Correction quickly becomes a distraction from the conversation your grandchild tries to have with you. Conversational correction looks a lot like this:

Grandchild:	Grandpa, we spent two hours at the swimming pool.
Grandma:	No, it was one-and-a-half hours.
Grandchild:	Okay. And I swam six laps on my own.
Grandma:	No, it was only four.
Grandchild:	Okay. Then we left to get a hamburger.
Grandma:	No, you had a hot dog.
Grandchild:	Okay, we came home, and I took a nap for an hour.
Grandma:	No, it was 30 minutes.

You get the picture from this conversation. What is it about people that they can't leave well enough alone and just let someone have a conversation without correcting any possible misinformation? What happens in these situations is that eventually the child will have a conversation only in the presence of one, avoiding the corrector's presence. Most grandkids would rather not share anything than have a discussion full of correction.

> Most grandkids would rather not share anything than have a discussion full of correction.

Bring Value to the Conversation

For years, so many grandparents held jobs where people listened, valued their opinions, and couldn't wait to hear what they had to say. Then they retire, and no one wants to listen to what they have to say. They feel like they've lost their value. They no longer contribute. They miss their positions of prestige they held in their pre-retirement years. Basically, they got pretty used to the praise and value they got from the interactions they had with people.

Perhaps retirement hasn't brought what you thought it would. If you miss the validation you used to get from your job, you may try to recoup it in your conversations with those around you now (usually your spouse, kids, and grandkids). Ask yourself how much of your conversation is an attempt to get value from the person you're communicating with rather than bringing value to them.

If this applies to you, I want you to know you don't have to prove your value. You are exempt from having to do so because you are a grandparent. You don't have to prove anything to anyone. You are already valued because of who you are. Your grandkids show you the value you hold by merely coming to you for wisdom, to ask questions, or to sit in your presence and hear your stories. You are more than important, more than valuable. You are invaluable.

Focus on Your Grandchildren

You've had a lifetime of people listening to you. It's your turn to listen to your grandchildren. I love this paraphrasing of scripture that I mentioned earlier.

> Spouting off before listening to the facts is both shameful and foolish. (Proverbs 18:13, NLT)

Let me ask you one more time. Do you listen, or do you just wait to talk?

Foolish grandparents hear something and, instead of trying to truly listen, respond quickly because they know the answer and want to be the first to hit the buzzer with the right answer. It's like they're on a game show competing with others. They have to win, and they have to be right. Many grandparents are more concerned with what their response will be than hearing their grandchildren's hearts behind their questions. They want to make sure they sound good rather than listening and interpreting well. They might be more intent on sharing their story than listening to their grandchildren's.

The best grandparents remember they've had a lifetime to be heard; now it's their grandchildren's turn.

Repeat Back What They Just Said

Remember the age difference between you and your grandkids I wrote about earlier? If you're striving to understand what they are saying, but you're not sure you get it, repeat what you hear back to them.

> "Okay, this is what I'm hearing you say. Am I getting it right?"
> "Is this what I'm hearing you communicate?"

It's an easy way to keep the discussion on track. It helps prevent you from wandering down conversational bunny trails. It ensures that you're picking up on the heart of what they want to say; while helping them put their feelings into words they might not even know how to say. Grandkids are dying for someone to listen and hear.

I know a young man named Mike who struggled at home. He

often said to me that he had a tough time finding someone who would just listen to him. Mike was not a bad kid. He just wanted to have a relationship with someone who would show a bit of compassion and empathy as he wrestled with normal adolescent issues.

He was one of those kids that thought a little more deeply than most teens. As a result, he felt things a little more deeply as well. Mike struggled with a little bit of depression. He rejected my suggestion of going to see a counselor so he would have someone to talk to. "They're always trying to fix me instead of listening to what I have to say," Mike said. He just wanted to be heard.

The best grandparents remember they've had a lifetime to be heard; now it's their grandchildren's turn.

In desperation, this young man got to the end of his rope, figuratively and literally. He tried to hang himself. Finally, that got the attention of those around him. He didn't die, but he did damage his spine to the point that he'll spend the rest of his life in a wheelchair. Mike told me that his unsuccessful attempt to kill himself was so that the people he loved would read the six-page letter he wrote describing what he was feeling and thinking all along. All Mike wanted was someone to listen. It almost cost his life.

Grandkids are dying for someone just to listen. Don't pay that awful price. Be the listening ear they need.

The fool speaks, the wise man listens.

—Ethiopian proverb

Chapter 20

Play it Smart; They're Watching

Let us not love with words or speech but with actions and in truth.
1 John 3:18

A ctions speak louder than words."
"It's not what you say; it's what you do."

"I can't hear what you're saying because your actions are speaking too loud."

You've heard these sayings before, I know. You can't live as long as we all have without finding some placard or post that encourages integrity and promotes truthfulness.

You will be known to your grandkids by what you do, not what you say you will do.

The question to answer would be, "Do the words out of my mouth match the actions my grandkids see in my life?"

When words and actions line up well, that's called integrity. The character traits of honesty, fairness, truthfulness, sincerity, and trustworthiness will be validated or invalidated by the actions they see. Be careful; they're watching.

In your grandkids' earlier years, they accept anything and everything you say. When they get into their teen years, observation becomes more important. They are beginning to understand that they live in a culture that offers them fake news, fake social structures, fake friends, and fake media. Remember what I mentioned before? Appearance and performance matter more than honesty and honor. Kids don't innately know the difference between counterfeit and real. They learn the difference from trial and error in their earlier adolescent years. This sets them on a course to seek out those relationships that are genuine and authentic.

It is my hope they find someone genuine and authentic in you. Be trustworthy grandparents who can be relied on to be true to their words and deeds.

Here is what I think integrity looks like for grandparents. There is a *vulnerability* that shows who you really are, coupled with a willingness to express emotion and identify your own hurts and struggles. I used to think the honor given to grandparents came because of their ability to hide their character flaws and escape observation by only visiting for short lengths of time. I thought grandparents smiled, doled out hugs and dollars, and never revealed their true selves. I now think otherwise.

Teens are intrinsically good at sniffing out fakes. They know when they're having the wool pulled over their eyes. Removing yourself from observation isn't the answer. Exposure of your true self is. The more they know about who you are, warts and all, the closer the relationship will be. Vulnerability entails being open about who you are. You admit struggles, confess failures, and disclose past mistakes. These confessions make you more human. If beloved grandparents failed and still came out okay, then grandchildren can fail and know they'll make it through.

I've met parents and grandparents who never wanted anyone to know they were married before. Many never let anyone know they had an abortion, smoked pot during college, or got fired from a job. Others hesitate to admit any failure, mistake, blunder, time spent in jail, or illegal activities. Lots of grandparents are cautious to admit past wrongdoing, never realizing that admission and confession clear the path for open and frank relationships. Some are never open about anything, and the mysteries of their lives are taken to their graves. When all faults remain hidden and pushed under the carpet, genuineness and authenticity never happen in a relationship.

Confidence would be another trait of integrity. When grandparents are confident, that confidence can be transferred to their grandchildren. It's about being comfortable in your own skin, not fearful of someone seeing the real deal. Vulnerability is about being open; confidence is an assuredness of who you are and Whose you are.

The trait of *honesty* can be seen when grandparents answer questions or when they ask someone else a question. People who are honest speak the truth in love, aren't going to let wrongdoings slide, and call a spade a spade without beating about the bush. Honesty can be seen when a grandmother admits and apologizes for the times she has gossiped or nagged. Honesty can be seen in a grandfather who admits the truth if asked by a grandson if he has ever had a problem with pornography. Honest people return what isn't theirs; answer questions truthfully, and never hide things. Honesty is the truth, the whole truth, and nothing but the truth.

Honest grandparents come clean long before they die. If there's been a *chink in the armor*, it's repaired before they go so their message and legacy remain intact. The hope they transferred to their grandkids rings true long after they're gone.

Responsibility for one's actions, past and present, is so important in the development of a healthy young adult. Good grandparents make sure they model responsibility, especially because their grandchildren are watching them. Grandparents who model responsibility show their loved ones they never have to worry about cleaning up any messes left behind when grandparents die. There is no unfinished business others have to take care of.

Responsibility means taking the skeletons out of the closet, accepting responsibility for them being there in the first place, and being vulnerable and honest enough to lay claim to what you have done. All this gives you the opportunity to share your story of your redemption.

Ones who are full of integrity are *secure* enough to speak their mind and stand up for what is right and true. These folks confront wrongdoing and don't tolerate the violation of their core principles.

They trust in themselves and their belief systems, and don't waste time worrying what others think. They are not swayed but remain steady. They know God is in control, so they don't have to be.

Another aspect of integrity is a *willingness to take risks*, not be afraid of failure. I'm not talking about financial investments or jumping out of an airplane. I'm talking about taking risks in relationships, confronting what is wrong, speaking the truth in love, exposing your past, risking your reputation for deeper relationship, and taking responsibility for wrongdoing when it may mean some type of consequence.

And lastly, grandparents with integrity *practice what they preach*. Period. They are the opposite of hypocrites and being two-faced. They eliminate falseness and any double standard and approach life with sincerity. Their words and actions never contradict.

How do you rate? Are you a grandfather or grandmother with integrity? Wherever you land on the scale, all the integrity in the world won't impact your grandkids unless you are involved in their lives and give them the opportunity to see you for who you are. Be around. Be steady. Be vulnerable. Be honest. Be responsible. You want your grandchildren to become men and women with integrity. You have to model it first. Your family's legacy largely depends on you.

> Your family's legacy largely depends on you.

Integrity takes consistency. You can't be one kind of grandmother in front of the grandkids and another kind of woman when they're not around. Your reputation will precede you. Double standards don't fly.

Here's a personal story. I travel a lot. I'm on and off planes every week speaking somewhere around the country. As a result, I've learned to travel well by myself and am pretty self-sufficient when it comes to planes, trains, and automobiles (and hotels). I can get where I need to go pretty easily and return home without any anxiety or strife because I've learned how to make it all work.

When I travel with others, I'm easily frustrated. They don't travel like I do. They obviously don't understand how this traveling thing works. They don't want to eat where I want to eat, don't follow my time schedule and my way of operating. How rude! Okay, in other words, I'm pretty self-centered when I travel.

I can ruin a vacation before we even get there, yet when I arrive at our destination, I can have a blast and enjoy the time with everyone. I'm not sure they enjoy the time with me because of the way I acted in the process of getting to our destination. It's not where you vacation, but how you get there that counts.

I need to be a man of integrity when I travel solo, and the same man of integrity when I travel with others, especially my family. I have to remind myself that how we get there is more important than the vacation itself, in terms of how they perceive me and accept my role in their lives.

I want my grandkids not to wait to say great things about me after I'm gone to my final destination. I want them to enjoy my presence as we travel together through this thing called life. The more genuine I am and the more authentic I can be make all the difference in how we travel together. Your grandkids need you to be their model of genuine and authentic. They need you, and they're watching your every move.

PART V — YOUR LEGACY

Chapter 21

A Legacy of Relationship

Therefore I intend always to remind you of these qualities, though you know them and are established in the truth that you have.

2 Peter 1:12 (ESV)

I can promise you these three things: You're going to die sometime after you read this book. It's going to happen sooner than you think. It's not going to happen the way you want it to happen.

There's something about embracing the inevitability of life ending one day that has a way of focusing you on what is most important today. It helps you live smarter and look at each day as a blessing. Yesterday I went to a restaurant and the waitress asked me, "Are you celebrating anything today?"

"Yes, I am," I said. "I woke up this morning, and that's worth celebrating."

If you're feeling that brisk fall wind of change ushering in a transition of the seasons in your life, then no doubt you are also wondering a bit about what your life has been about. You start to focus on what will be remembered about you once you are gone. Some folks don't care, and when they are gone they will quickly be forgotten, except for an occasional search on Ancestry.com or when some relative is flipping through old family photos.

Then there are those of us who want to pass something on. We want to know our lives meant something more than mere existence. We want to see how we made an impact on someone else. We want to make lives better and our time on earth significant. We want to know we made a difference.

I'm not sure I thought about this when my own kids were born. Jan and I were so ecstatic about having kids (and scared to death) that we only thought about how we were going to survive. We were both twenty-one years old, managing apartments, going to school fulltime, and working two jobs while leading a Young Life club for kids. When Melissa and Adam were born, we saw a miracle happen before our eyes. We never regretted having kids early, but we weren't focusing on our legacy back then.

> Your legacy will be written in two places—your tombstone and in the hearts of those who know you.

When our grandkids were born, we encountered new feelings of getting older, wanting to make an impact, and thinking about life from a different perspective. Our kids changed the way we lived; our grandkids changed our hearts and our focus.

There was something so different about having grandkids that my whole perspective on life changed. It was no longer about making money, doing a great job, building a career, and involving myself in everything good I could find. It was more about impact, knowing these little kids I was holding, who would eventually call me Poppa, are the ones who would carry on any family legacy if there was going to be one. They were the hope for future generations of our family. It was then that I asked myself, *What do you want to be known for?*

Short of making the history books, setting records, or committing some heinous crime, most of us will be forgotten when our grandkids are gone. Our work may be remembered, something we wrote or videotaped may be read or viewed, but our legacy will only extend as far as our relationships with our grandkids.

Your legacy will be written in two places. One is on your

tombstone. Now, I don't know about you, but I don't know many people who run around cemeteries with the intent of gathering wisdom from the one-liners on tombstones. This headstone monument thing seems a bit overrated to me. People always ask me what I want written as my epitaph, like there's going to be thousands of people visiting my buried carcass to see what my life was about. I really don't care what's on my marker. I'm sure it will say when I was born and when I died, like all the neighbors planted in my new neighborhood.

Okay, I'm digressing a bit here, but after a funeral, when do you ever see a person's headstone again? When you're laying another family member to rest, but that's really not the best time to be searching for some tombstone wisdom. So I don't think too much about what will be chiseled about me after I'm gone.

The second place your legacy will be written is in the hearts of those who know you. In particular, those you have known.

A legacy is not about depositing a few gold nuggets of wisdom that will be remembered by all. You're not a box of fortune cookies—clever but not very deep. A legacy is not just doing a whole lot of good for others. A real legacy is the connection you made with family through the deep relationships you had with them. A legacy is found within the hope and wisdom you passed down to your children and grandchildren, the truths they can pass down to the next generation. Grandparents who leave a legacy are not only remembered for what they contributed, but also for the life-giving qualities they provided to those around them.

My main concern is not everyone out there. My main concern is the health and welfare of my own family. That's where I want to make the most difference, in the lives of my wife, my kids (including son- and daughters-in-law, even though I can't tell the difference between because I consider them all the same), and my grandkids.

I've been to many funerals, and it's interesting to see who attends. When my mom died, the people that attended were a few of her friends, a couple from her Sunday school, a couple of neighbors, and a few folks from some of the organizations where she volunteered. The remaining people there were all family. Our whole family was there. The attendance at funerals speaks loudly to the legacy that deceased person left for their family.

All the wisdom shared through your legacy, should it go any further than your life, will go as far as your grandkids or great-grandkids. That's good enough for me.

I'll leave it to the next generation to take care of their grandkids; I'm just trying to keep up with the four I have.

My point in all this is to ask you, "What do you want to be known for?" My real hope is you'll ask that question for yourself. Then answer it and live the answer.

I think about that when I'm introduced to people, run into acquaintances, and when someone introduces me to an audience before I speak. I've been described to crowds and individuals in so many ways that many times I chuckle and think, "Is this really how they see me?" At least a few times I've cocked my head and asked, "Is this really what I want to be known for?"

I was recently at a Texas Rangers baseball game and ran into a fellow named Aaron Watson. He's a country music artist and a great fellow. He introduced me to his wife as, "Honey, this is the guy that sends us that pecan pie for Christmas every year."

Many people just know me as "Jan's husband." Others introduce me as, "This is Mark, and he's the guy that lives with all those kids in East Texas." Some remember me as, "That guy with the mustache." Many of our Heartlight parents introduce me to their friends as, "He's the one I was telling you about that cooks those great steaks." When speaking at seminars or conferences, I'm known as "That guy on the radio."

A few weeks ago, Amy Grant introduced me to her husband Vince Gill. I was excited to finally meet him. Amy and Vince are warm, genuinely kind people. No joke, her introduction was, "Vince, this is the guy who lives with those struggling teens and has all those cabins that are joined by walkways." I'm not kidding.

I can see it on my tombstone now: "Here lies Mark, the pie guy on the radio who has a mustache and lives with all those kids, who is married to Jan and cooks a great steak and has cabins all joined by walkways."

Not exactly what I was going for in my legacy. Not quite what I want to be known for.

I know this: Legacy is all about relationships. Not just my relationship with my grandkids, but my grandkids' relationships with me. I want to know them, and I want to be known by them.

I recently heard a young lady who stated simply, "Stop trying to be there for me when you know nothing about me." It reminded me that having an impact on someone doesn't just happen because we know them, or when we do something that can benefit their life. It's all about relationship, about getting to know them and know them well. It's communicating life across a bridge of relationship that doesn't stop if they don't respond. It's offering your life to them regardless of what comes back to you.

Legacy is all about relationships.
Relationships matter.

Family relationships are tricky. I've heard many families tell me they can all get along if they don't talk about religion or politics. Others tell me that as long as they don't bring up other certain topics, then the holidays will go well. I've always thought relationships have to be more than that. Relationships, true relationships, don't need to be bound by restrictions but rather be freed up to flourish.

If you're going to have freedom within your relationships, then you might have to accept the fact that it's okay to disagree. At times you may be polar opposites, but your relationship can still thrive.

Your relationship with your grandkids can be the most important relationship they have during their teen years. Don't mess it up by requiring your grandkids to believe, act, and present themselves the way you do. The relationship is always the most important thing, because if you don't have a relationship, then you will never be able to have those much-needed discussions that might bring about a different way of thinking. You'll never have talks to disperse the wisdom you have accumulated. You'll eliminate the chance to have influence and opportunity to shape their thinking and mold their values.

Grandparents, even if you don't accept the lifestyle and choices your grandchildren make, don't *throw the baby out with the bath water*. If you do, you won't have a chance to touch the hearts of those who long for your presence in their lives.

I meet kids all the time who are involved in activities I don't approve of. I hear teens spouting off comments and beliefs I'll never embrace. I see people living lifestyles I don't agree with. I meet with girls who are making stupid decisions with their bodies, who are engaged in activities that are immoral at best and destructive at worst. I see young men making poor choices and countering anything that resembles biblical standards and moral principles.

I can reject them and their lifestyles and never have an influence, or I can love them right where they are and hope to steer them in another direction. I'll say it one more time. Accepting them does not mean that I accept their choices, lifestyle, behaviors, or actions. I'm not condoning when I don't correct. I can love them in spite of their behaviors. I know actions are an expression of their hearts, and that's what I want to influence.

Relationship matters.

Regardless of the differences of opinions or the inconsistencies in your beliefs, the relationships with your grandchildren matter. You can have an amazing impact on the lives of your grandkids even when your beliefs are miles apart because you are the one who can offer the hope and help they are desperately looking for. You have the ability to leave a legacy no one else can. Leave a good one, filled with family members who remember in detail the positive impact your life had on them. It's a pay-it-forward kind of thing. Just as others had an impact on you and changed your life, I'm sure you have a desire to have an impact on others.

Legacies don't just happen. They're made. Keep making yours today. If you haven't started yet, there's no time to waste.

Chapter 22

Supporting your Grandkid's Parents

And let us consider how we may spur one another
on toward love and good deeds.
Hebrews 10:24 (NIV)

Perhaps like you, I always thought I was a pretty good parent. I attended every event possible, loved my kids, provided what was needed, and made sure they survived their toddler and teen years. When I became a grandparent, my instinct was to do the same thing I had done well in my parenting years.

There isn't a grandparent out there who wouldn't support the concept that kids need a parent, not another friend. And there isn't a parent out there who wouldn't support the notion that grandchildren need grandparents, not another parent.

The minute a grandparent crosses the imaginary boundary that divides the roles of parents and grandparents, they violate basic principles of family structure. Grandparents who act like the parents when the parents are right there in the picture, cause confusion and conflict. Eventually, the power struggle between the two generations divides families.

There are situations where grandparents must intervene and

sometimes take over. That occurs when physical, medical, legal, or mental issues incapacitate their children, or when death, drugs, or divorce have created an unsafe atmosphere for their grandkids. I know many dear grandmas and grandpas who have to parent the second generation. While I don't think they would choose to be in that position, they willingly assume the role of sacrifice to provide a better life for their grandkids.

I would eagerly and gladly shoulder the parental role should my grandchildren's parents (my kids) become debilitated, disabled, or unwilling to parent for some reason. I'd assume this role, but it wouldn't be a position I would choose. It's family, so I would accept and embrace it. Because they are my grandkids, I would do anything to help.

That responsibility in the face of adversity is far different than what I mean here. I'm talking about well-meaning grandparents who step in where they're not needed or wanted by acting more like a parent than a grandparent to their grandchildren. I'm talking about grandparents who undermine their daughter or son because they think they can do a better job or feel like the parents aren't accomplishing what is needed in raising their grandkids.

I never had a grandparent involved in my life, so I wasn't quite sure what my role was supposed to be when I became one. I never had an uncle involved in my life; that's why I'm probably not a good uncle. I'm not altogether sure what role they play in a family. Since I had no grandparent to model myself after when I became a grandparent, I had to figure out quickly what my new role would be. Being a grandparent doesn't mean I parent my grandkids grandly or on a greater scale. It means I have a new role that has something to offer of grander proportions.

When grandparents complement and assist what parents are charged by God with doing, the tide for teens can turn.

Grandparents possess the power of influence in the lives of their grandchild, but it hurts, not helps, if they wield that power by trying to be the parent. Undermining parents drive a wedge between you and your kids. That wedge then divides you from your grandchildren. You can help shape your grandchildren, but only by coming alongside their parents.

If you only offer the role of a parent, then your grandkids will never have the opportunity to benefit from the presence of grandparents in their lives. If you've never been a grandparent before and you don't know how, don't assume it's just a continuation of your parenting skills and capabilities. It's a completely different role.

> You can help shape your grandchildren, but only by coming alongside their parents.

Some grandparents want to prove something to their kids, so they try to make up through their grandkids whatever they missed or messed up during their parenting years. In their eyes, all can be made right by grandparenting like a parent. They can right past wrongs by pouring their misguided parenting energies into their grandkids. It doesn't work.

You may have to accept the fact that maybe you weren't a great parent. Grandchildren do not offer you the chance to redeem yourself in that department. Remember, it's not about you.

When I think about how I really was while my kids were growing up, sometimes I think we were all just trying to survive. School, work, ministry, more work, time away from home, and never enough money. Those were hard years spent mostly trying to keep everything together. I think I landed on the borderline between being an okay parent and a good parent. I'm not sure I ever hit pretty good.

If you weren't a good parent, you can't go back and be a good parent with your grandchildren. You can be an excellent and effective grandparent. You can't go back and do the same things a parent would, but you can move into a new role that can greatly benefit your grandchildren.

I warn you now and will share more points later. The minute you begin to contradict, undermine, or badmouth your kids (your grandkids' parents), either by word or by action, you cause more problems than you fix.

I've seen this story hundreds of times. A grandparent believes that a mom or dad isn't handling the kids (their grandkids) in an appropriate way. The grandparent then stops supporting the parents and offers to help, telling the grandkids they can move in—against the mom or dad's desire. It sets up a dynamic very similar to co-parenting after divorce, where loyalties are divided, and children can manipulate everyone involved. No one wins when there is competition amongst the primary adult figures in a teen's life. A good guy/bad guy dynamic develops, with frustrated parents and misguided grandparents.

Now, I think there are times when a cooling-off period is needed between parents and teens, and the decision to have a child stay with grandma and grandpa for a time may be a good thing. It's good only when the parents and grandparents are on the same page, so the already struggling teen can't play one side against the other and get away with murder. It is not a good thing if the grandparents don't or won't support the parents.

I recall one family in particular. A mother was having a tough time with her son because the teen had such a winning personality that he had become quite the con artist. This was a side of their grandson the grandparents had never seen. The parents decided on a course of action to help bring their son back in line with their family principles. Of course, the son balked at the idea of having to make changes in his life and complained in his best winning manner to the higher ups—his grandparents. As well intended as could be but without consulting the parents, they offered their grandson a chance to come live with them. Big no-no. The grandson now had a way out and no longer had to make changes in his life. And the grandparents, not seeing what was really going on because they had been conned by this loving grandson, provided his escape and almost ruined the family in the process.

Mom and dad felt invalidated. The son got out of assuming responsibility, and the grandparents' offer drove a stake in the relationships within the family. Provision for their grandson quickly turned into enabling. The grandson in his new environment was able to continue his foolish behavior. Honestly, the grandson was lucky he didn't lose his life. His grandparents' good intentions merely extended this young man's walk on the wild side.

The grandson used and manipulated grandparents to get what he wanted. He said all the right words to convince them he was on the up and up. The grandchild's outward appearance of good behavior was just a smokescreen to blind his grandparents into thinking he was doing okay. In reality, the grandparents' inability to see their grandson in his true light fueled his negative behavior and gave him time to go deeper and deeper into the dark hole he was digging for himself.

The grandparents thought they were helping, and all they were doing was making a bigger mess for his parents to one day have to deal with more strongly. Everyone lost, all because the grandparents thought they could do better than this young man's parents.

Can grandparents do a better job than parents in raising the grandkids? Well, sure they can. I know I can. Grandparents have prior experience. They can repeat their successes and have learned from their mistakes. In their day, kids *knew better* than to behave like their grandkids might be behaving, and they believe they can nip those behaviors right in the bud.

Grandparents must be doing an awesome job, because all I see on their Facebook walls and in annual Christmas cards are the wonderful pictures they post and send of everyone all smiles and full of laughter. For the most part, a grandparent's role is to be the fun guy (or gal). They don't have to and should not deal with all the mess.

What I don't see in these happy photos are the everyday interactions where conflicts, confrontations, disagreements, fights, struggles over homework, poor choices, completing chores, and little skirmishes on the battlefront of family life are the reality. These paint a better and much more accurate picture of a home intent on helping teens get through their adolescent years alive and with some measure of relationship intact when a child reaches maturity.

In the case mentioned earlier, the grandparents eventually saw the light, the same one the parents had seen for months, and they then became a part of the solution rather than adding to the present problems.

They got on board with the parents and presented a united front to their grandson so he couldn't maneuver around any of them. These wiser grandparents now supported the parents even if they didn't agree with their methods, their style, or their requests for their child. They assumed their rightful place of being the grandparents they needed to be.

If your kids come to you and ask for help when they are struggling with your grandkids, that's a different story. In that scenario, grandparents are being invited to be involved in the process of helping when all parental efforts have been exhausted. Grandparents may then take on a short-term, more parental role in the life of the struggling grandchild, but it's with the parents' consent. Everyone is on the same page, so there's no wiggle room for the teen's rebellion to grow. There's a far different attitude about grandparents' involvement when they have been issued an invitation by the parents, rather than barging their way in.

Your home may be a haven for your grandkids, but that doesn't mean it's a free-for-all for selfish behavior. When my grandkids come to my home, there are home rules. However, if they violate the home rules, I am limited in my authority to dole out consequences. If a grandchild breaks one of the house boundaries, grandparents don't usually have the authority to ground a child, take away their car, or park their cell phone for a few days. At least not without asking the parents' permission first.

Grandparents do have the authority to either report the infraction to parents (especially in the earlier years of a grandchild's life) or tell grandkids they are welcome in their home as long as certain rules are adhered to. You don't have to be used and abused by anyone. My suggestion for you is to require respect, honesty, and obedience conveyed on pictures, placards, and signs hanging on your walls and talked about around your dinner table. Say things like the following:

"Hey, I want you to know that we honor *respect* as a strength, as most disrespect comes from a place of weakness."

"Guys, above anything else my hope is that you will always be full of *honesty*. Telling the truth sometimes hurts people, but being dishonest to people will only hurt them deeper."

"Hey, listen up. I'm not asking for much, but I am asking you trust me on this one and be in *obedience* to what I'm saying, even if you don't agree with me."

When you communicate these principles, you do so as a grandparent. Your appeal to them relies on the strong relationships you develop with them. Present your principles in the form of short lessons, bits of wisdom, and traits you hope they pick up from you while in your presence.

> When you support your grandkid's parents, they will be more apt to come ask for help and seek your counsel.

By supporting your son or daughter as the parent, you use your influence as one who is speaking from the outside. This is really a position of strength, as you don't have to correct. In reality, you don't have to be involved in the lives of your grandchildren at all. You choose to do so. This shows your grandchildren you want to be in a special relationship with them. No one can make you. It's your choice. When they see this, it gives you a voice they won't find elsewhere.

When you support your grandkids' parents, they will be more apt to come ask for help and seek your counsel. You will be seen as participating teammates rather than adversarial foes, thus giving you more of a say in the lives of your grandkids and a stronger relationship with your adult kids.

When you think your kids have it wrong when it comes to your grandkids, here's what you can do right.

Don't parent when you're not the parent. Be the grandparent.

I don't agree with every way my kids parent their children. There are many times I think I'd have even better grandkids if their parents would just follow my line of thought. I've had my tongue replaced twice as I've bitten it so many times wanting to suggest a better way. After all,

I write books and speak on this stuff every day.

Then I remember the parenting gig is all theirs. Not mine. I had my turn. Yes, I think they're on their iPads and cell phones too much. Yes, they should get those kids out of diapers and quit sticking that pacifier plug in their mouth. Yes, they shouldn't say certain words around them. Yes, they should push them in some areas and quit pushing so hard in others. Yes, they should make them clean up more and quit making messes. Yes, they should help them understand how great we are as grandparents.

They just don't do this parenting thing as I did and would do again. The reason? Because God placed my grandkids in my kids' care to parent, not in mine. He gave me kids to parent, and if I did such a great job then why don't I trust my kids to repeat it now with my grandkids? Ultimately, I do trust them. We just do things differently. So I'll keep my mouth shut, keep biting my tongue, and trust that God knows what He's doing. And I'll pray He helps me become the grandparent He's created me to be.

Support your kid's parenting styles and desires.

Styles will always be different. Your kids say the same thing all of us have said, "I don't want to parent my kids the way my parents parented me." They're doing it differently because they learned some things from you that they don't want to carry on.

Just as you are trying to honor the position God placed you in, they are honoring the position He put them in. Maybe God is encouraging your kids to raise their kids in a certain way. Be careful. Your lack of support may actually be a lack of support for God's plan for their lives.

You need to do your thing and do it well. Let your kids do theirs with all your support.

Don't undercut your kids.

You more than likely can give bigger gifts. You can do some things for your grandkids that your kids can't. You have the means to do it better. You're probably more relaxed than your kids and could easily provide a relationship the kids would enjoy more than spending time with their own parents.

You could. But it may not be a wise move. One of your roles as a grandparent is to develop a strong relationship with your grandchildren, but never so you can take away from the relationship that they are to have with their parents.

As a matter of fact, you should be helping your grandkids love and strengthen their bonds with their parents more and more and more.

Support your kids even in your disagreement.

This may mean you help your grandchild understand your role by saying, "Even though I don't agree with your mom, I do support her. I always have, and I always will. You guys need to work this one out, and I'll help where I can. However, I won't go against what she says."

Offer a place of relief and rest, not escape.

Offer that place of rest where they feel safe and can be refreshed and rekindled, but not a place where they escape the consequences of their behavior or elude and avoid the responsibilities put on them. At any age, a child would much rather avoid a painful situation. I encourage you to provide a place where they don't avoid the pain of life, but learn to navigate through the agony and heartache of growing up.

Give advice only when asked.

Even a fool appears wise when he keeps his mouth shut. Have you read that a few times throughout this book? It's a wise proverb that bears repeating, and repeating, and repeating some more.

Don't badmouth by words or actions.

Let your grandkids know of your parental struggles. Make your kids (their parents) appear normal, not as villains. Don't do anything in secret except for surprise birthday parties and anniversary celebrations. The minute you say, "Don't tell your mom this," or "Don't let your dad know," you are bad-mouthing their parents. You are not respecting their position. You are showing you don't have to give your support.

Sometimes your actions speak louder than words.

Send them on a vacation to spend time together without you.

It's fun to spend time with grandkids, but I encourage you to help your kids make some memories with your grandkids as well. Give them fun times away from your presence.

While you want to communicate and you want to share with your grandchildren, don't ever forget whose kids they really are. You have been given a chance to be involved in the lives of these teens who don't belong to you. It's a blessing! You get to participate in the fun without all the dirty work anymore. You know what? I enjoy my grandkids, and I never changed one of their diapers. When they get sick, I let them go throw up somewhere else. When they're in trouble, they get to answer to someone else. When they pull some stupid stunt, it's all on their parents. I get to sit back and enjoy the good times; parents have to deal with all the rotten stuff.

So try to give them a break from the day in, day out routine. Help them enjoy their kids and have some fun. It's easy for grandparents to be a killjoy of fun within the family if the fun is all about having it around grandparents. Show your support for your kids by blessing them and granting them the opportunity to spend some time as a family and make some great memories.

Don't ever believe you know best because you don't.

You don't live with the struggling grandchild every day. You may not be able to detect bluffing behavior during occasional visits. Your grandkids may be sweet as honey to you and be a living nightmare for mom or dad. Your grandkids' parents need your support, not abandonment or criticism.

You are to give a bigger-picture view, yes. You are to give perspective. But that doesn't mean you see everything happening. I hear parents mention to me all the time that their parents would never understand because they don't see the half of it and wouldn't believe it if they did. As mentioned before, I can change spark plugs in a car, but

I can't replace the engine. I'm not the expert on that engine. I simply don't see the whole picture of how everything works, connects, and functions together properly. You may see a little, but that doesn't mean you understand it all. Don't charge in as an expert. Go to your kids in humility, offering to listen and be available to answer anything they ask.

Your grandkids' parents need your support, not abandonment or criticism.

The grandparenting role becomes a confusing mess when grandma and grandpa go outside the boundaries and become something they were not designed to be. You must support your kids whenever they're doing it right, and support them, even more, when you think they're doing it wrong. Even if you could do it better, it wouldn't be better if it were not your place.

Don't offer an escape for your grandchild's foolishness, but instead provide a consistent message of being a part of your family team. You can be a source of wisdom for your grandkids and their parents, but only if you know your role and understand and support their role.

Chapter 23

Making Memories Before You Lose Yours

And I will make every effort to see that after my departure
you will always be able to remember these things.
2 Peter 1:15

The question that looms for many grandparents in their time of reflection is, "What do I want to be known for?" Maybe the more important question is, "How will they remember me?" It's not necessarily what you want to be known for that counts, but how they will recount their times with you.

It's been said that the moods of a lifetime can be found in the all-but-forgotten experiences of adolescence. That doesn't mean that vacation or trip together before adolescence is nonexistent in the memories of your grandchildren. It just means those remembered the most clearly and enjoyed the most will be the ones taken between the ages of twelve to twenty.

One of my greatest fears is that when I die, the money I saved and invested gets distributed to my family, and I didn't get to spend it on creating experiences while I was with them. I don't want to miss these moments because I am too darn busy. Money sure hasn't been my focus, but I saved diligently so Jan and I would be taken care of in our later years. Now I'm more concerned with the memories in my family's hearts than I am the amount of money in my bank account.

I was recently reminded of the futility of gathering and collecting everything we do in life, knowing that none of it can be taken with us when we die. I attended the funeral of my dear friend David Muth after he succumbed to his fight with Parkinson's. I arrived in Indiana for his funeral and walked in after the service began. I was ushered to the front to sit with his wife and daughters. I sat through the service holding the hands of his girls and looking at him in the casket. As I walked up to see my friend, I noticed that his wife Amy had put memorabilia of sorts in the casket propped up around David—pictures of times together, items that stirred memories with this wonderful man, and a few trinkets that meant nothing to most, yet were invaluable to the family. It was touching, to say the least, and my eyes kept dripping on the casket as I recalled the wonderful times we had together.

What was not there in the casket was money. No cash, no checkbook, nor were there any pictures of dollar bills. No car, no valuable possessions were being buried with him. When we loaded him up for the graveside, there was no U-Haul attached to his hearse. Just him and the beautiful memories he created for his family.

If you can't take any of it with you, then spend it on experiences that last a lifetime and leave a legacy. Spend times together that bind the hearts in relationship together. This crazy disease took away David's time here on earth, but it couldn't take away his family's beautiful memories of their times together. Though painful to remember, those memories are, and always will be, wonderfully inscribed on the hearts of those he loved.

Money is a great inheritance. It's a bonus, a gift, a blessing from left field, usually not anticipated and always greatly appreciated. However, why wait until you're gone to share a little of it?

I was reminded of how a little went a long way when I gave my granddaughter twenty dollars to support a car wash that she was participating in. She was so grateful and excited that I helped. A simple twenty-dollar bill…that's all it took to let her know I cared about what she cared about. For me, it was a reminder to her that when she needs something, I want her to come to me to ask. That doesn't keep her from going to her own parents or others she knows, but it affirms our relationship in a way that will keep her coming back for more than just money.

One of these days, I'm going to write checks for ten thousand dollars and give one to each of my grandkids. It's one of my goals. It is founded on a wish I had that was never fulfilled. When Jan and I were first married, we had no money. We struggled to make ends meet. It was a great date night if we were able to air-pop some popcorn and sit and watch a movie. I painted apartments in the evening, cleaned toilets, unclogged drains, worked two jobs, and was ecstatic when Young Life decided to pay me twenty-five dollars a month as I volunteered.

At one point, I remember we had a health insurance payment due of twenty-two dollars. I took my high school ring to a pawnshop and got twenty-three dollars for it. I paid the bill and ended up with one dollar in my pocket. I remember thinking, *I just wish someone would help us in some way.* We had a baby due, I was a student at Tulsa University, and Jan dropped out of nursing school because of morning sickness.

That's when I said to myself, *One of these days, I'm going to give some money to my grandkids at just the right time.* Now I'm thinking, *Why not?* I might as well give it to them while I'm alive and enjoy their excitement and pleasure than wait until I'm gone and everything is divvied up among my heirs anyway. Here's the only catch I'll put with the money. Each of my grandkids will be charged with giving the same amount to their own grandchildren one day when those grandkids need it the most. It's kind of a pay-it-forward deal, the start of a new tradition for our family.

The inheritance you leave is about more than dollars; it's about leaving an impact on your grandkids.

Chances are, by the time my kids get my inheritance, they really won't need it. They'll be making their own living and making ends meet. But unexpected windfalls give you the chance to do things, go places, or experience something you might not budget for otherwise. If I can give them that joy, why not give it now?

The inheritance you leave is about more than dollars; it's about leaving an impact on your grandkids. Events and occasions that trigger memories are important. These open the door to the life skills you shared, the legacy you built in their lives, and remind them of the special relationship you had with them.

When your grandchildren remember you, what will they remember you for?

The experiences with you are important. They open the doors to the hearts of your grandchild. My family has wonderful memories of going to the beach. After I'm buried or burnt, I hope that every time my family is at the beach they remember my love for the ocean, the wind, the waves, and the sea life we all enjoyed watching together. Those are great memories, but I want them to recall more than just, *Hey, remember how Poppa loved the beach?*

My wife Jan has populated East Texas with birds, as she feeds them every day. We have every type of bird you can imagine darting in and out of our backyard on a daily basis. Friends give her bird towels, bird glasses, bird gifts, and bird emblems. She's known as the bird lady. If that's all she's known as, that's kind of weird. If people think of Jan when they see a bird and remember nothing else about her, then her legacy will pass quickly and soon be forgotten.

But I think Jan is creating much more of a legacy. I think when friends and loved ones see birds, they will think of Jan. When they think of her and the memories they have of her, they'll also remember her love of animals, her ability to talk to anyone, her fun-loving personality, her strength through pain, her ability to listen well, her efforts to make everyone's life better, the lessons she taught, her love for God, and her ability to share how she found so much in Him. They'll think about how she laughed in the face of conflict, how she gave generously, and how her words were full of wisdom. They'll remember all of these things because even a bunch of feathery friends stir memories of deeper connections of who she really was to others.

Do you have memories built up in the hearts of your grandkids that will remind them of you? It's never too late to start.

Twenty years ago I had this crazy idea to pile up all the Christmas trees from all the houses at Heartlight and burn them on New Year's Eve. The next year we stuffed some fireworks in the trees. The following year we added gasoline. Every year, the blaze gets bigger and bigger. This family tradition has now turned into a community event. People come from everywhere to see the Christmas tree burning at the Gregston's place. It's a memory that will be with our family for years.

Now, I'm not suggesting you do the same. I don't know where you live, and you might get in trouble doing something in the city we habitually do in the country. I do suggest you create something memorable, magnificent, and meaningful to your family.

Think about what smells remind your grandkids of you? Is it that special candle you always burn, the perfume or cologne you wear, or the smell of your cooking at various times of the year? Whenever I smell boiling shrimp, I think of my dad. Is there a smell that is just unique to your home that reminds them of you? We had a young lady at Heartlight a couple of years ago that made a statement reflecting on her memory of home. She said she would occasionally go into her closet and open up her suitcase so she could *get a whiff of home*. The scent reminded her of what she missed dearly.

Start some traditions around your home. Perhaps it is leaving a jigsaw puzzle on the dining room table for everyone to gather and piece together. Maybe it's nights around the fireplace where everyone just catches up. Have you thought of having a joke night around the dinner table every Saturday night? Popping a champagne bottle on New Year's Eve? Or eating a special cultural meal to remind you of your heritage?

What is unique about you that you could teach your grandchild? Do you play a musical instrument? If so, purchase one for your grandchild and help them learn. Teach them how to do carpentry, operate a tractor, use some tools, build something, repair fence line, or care for and feed some animals. (Can you tell we live in the country?) Find one of your skills and talents and teach it to another.

Find a lifelong sport or activity you can do with your grandchild. I'm talking about golf, tennis, horseback riding, weight lifting or working out, shooting guns at a gun range, hunting, or any activity that can be done throughout the rest of your grandkids' lives. Schedule a time to go on a mission trip with your grandchild or volunteer somewhere local on a regular basis together. Go somewhere they'll go with no one else and keep a laid-back schedule that isn't filled with constant activity, so you have plenty of time for personal interaction.

Take a vacation and invite the whole family. When you go, eat a special meal that second night (after all have rested up) and share with them the beauty of family and how you want this trip to be an annual event.

Take a grandchild or two to an event that wows them, a concert of a favorite artist, a backstage experience, a Broadway musical, or a big sports event. My granddaughter Maile and I have gone to the Country Music Awards each year for eight years now. We even attended the CMA Festival in Nashville this year, and I let her bring a couple of her friends. It will be an annual event for us as long as she wants to go and I am able. I really can't afford to do that, but I can't afford *not* to.

Where would your granddaughter or grandson love to go? Why not make plans to take them?

What do you do on special holidays? Is there a ritual around your home? Is there a tradition to eat a Thanksgiving meal and then watch football or soccer all afternoon? Do you go to a Christmas Eve service, come home and open presents, and then spend Christmas afternoon going to a newly released movie?

If your grandkids only occasionally visit, make sure you have some things lined up for activities. As they get older, plan on some time where all can sit around and talk—not just be entertained. Go horseback riding, take a walk on the beach, ride ATV's around somewhere, shoot skeet in someone's field, or go to the symphony or a play and then out to eat.

Plan a fishing or hunting trip of a lifetime or a shopping spree in a place your grandkids have never been. Go to a tropical island or take that trip to Disneyworld you've always wanted to take. If you can't go, send others so they can have a wonderful experience.

Do something special on birthdays, the beginning of school, graduations, and weddings. Make it special by your attendance, but also provide something for those events that makes them—and your participation in them—memorable.

Spend time around a fireplace or an open fire on a cold night, whether it is in your backyard, on a beach, or on a mountaintop. Make it special.

Have a week where you entertain the grandkids when they come spend time with you. Make those memories by cooking great meals and wearing you out showing them they are special. When you can no longer do that at your home, go someplace else to make it happen.

These are all memory makers that will bring you to mind. When you're gone and there is a trigger that reminds them of you, it will prompt them to recall the loving impact you had on their life.

Personally, I love the idea and thought that my grandkids will remember me every time they smell the burning of powder and see the beauty of rockets, explosives, and fireworks. I'm sure those will bring a smile to their faces as they remember all the times we burnt up some Christmas trees and ushered in the New Year.

Make some memories before you lose yours.

But that's not the only thing I want them to remember about me. I want that memory and other memories of me to remind them of the wisdom I shared along the way. I want them to recall and put to good use in their lives the particular and specific nuggets of truth demonstrated and lived out by the way I treated them and the way they saw me treat other people.

Make some memories before you lose yours.

The remembrance of your generosity and kindness will last many lifetimes.

Yes, memories of you will last. Make sure they are good ones. This is the time of life to make sure all unfinished business gets taken care of. Is there something hidden in your closet? Are there skeletons that might come out after you pass away that could taint the memories of your good times together with your family? Is anything currently unresolved between you and any family members? Come clean and take care of the business of forgiveness and making amends now.

Don't leave your family hurting, wishing things could have been different, and talking about you negatively later. Is there something you are hiding about yourself from others? Could there be some unspoken pain that, if brought out in the open, would help everyone understand why things are the way they are? Are there habits, past or present, which need to be addressed so there are no surprises after you're gone? Are you fearful about some things in your past that you really don't think God is big enough to handle? God's Word tells us that's just not true.

> Even to your old age and gray hairs I am he, I am he who will sustain you. I have made you and I will carry you; I will sustain you and I will rescue you. (Isaiah 46:4)

I encourage you to leave this world with a clean slate. Tell it all, my friend. Tell it all. Tell the truth, the whole truth, and nothing but the truth. Make sure that no word can be said about you that is contrary to what everyone already knows, so your legacy will not be stained by something you left hidden during your life that is discovered after you're gone.

Those conversations are hard, but they are essential to a legacy that is spotless and unblemished. They might begin like this:

- Your grandmother and I have something to tell you.
- I want you to know that I'm not perfect.
- There are some things in my life you don't know about.
- I don't want you to hear these things from anyone else.
- I've been to some places and done some things you don't know about.

- There are some things in our family I want you to know about so they go no further.
- Knowing what I know may help you see things in a different light.
- I want you to know I haven't been totally honest with you.
- I didn't get to where I am without making some mistakes along the way.
- Poor choices haunted me earlier in life; I don't want you to make the same mistakes.

Clear the air, admit wrongdoings, ask for forgiveness, and strive to make your relationships right.

Many fear that the admission of wrongdoing will ruin a legacy and stain a memory beyond repair. Quite the contrary. What you will do by admitting your mistakes and failures is give your family members permission to clean out theirs. Through this, you usher in a world of hope for your grandkids and freedom in your family. You lay the groundwork for mental, emotional, and spiritual health. They'll remember the fun times, but also your admission of wrongdoing will be burned in their hearts forever. Not in a way that taints their memory of you, but in a way that causes them to remember your strength of character. Funny, isn't it? The hope will be ushered into the lives of your grandchildren not through your perfection, but through your imperfections.

They will remember you in the following ways:

- Remember when Grandpa shared about his life and let us know we, too, can make it?
- Remember when Grandma admitted her problem with anger and let us know why that existed in her life?
- Remember when Grandpa told us the truth about our family?
- Remember when Grandma shared with us how important it is not to hide anything?
- Remember when Grandpa cried and shared about his hurt and his poor choices?

- Remember when Grandma told us what really happened?
- Remember when Grandma and Grandpa gave us all hope and let us know that we're all going to be okay?

Go make memories before you lose yours. Leave a legacy of hope and influence.

Chapter 24

Transferring What You Believe to be Important

Having so fond an affection for you, we were well-pleased to impart to you not only the gospel of God but also our own lives, because you had become very dear to us.
1 Thessalonians 2:8 (NASB)

Most people don't know that in 1969, I was the Oklahoma Bible Quiz champ, after memorizing hundreds of scriptures as a ninth grader in Tulsa. I have always believed in hiding God's Word in my heart, for I know that out of the abundance of the heart his mouth speaks, at least that what scripture says (Luke 6:45, NKJV). In reflection, I think it's been my way of expressing my love for God and my commitment to Christ.

Others express themselves in various ways. Many preach. Some are great people of prayer. Some really get into worship. There are many diligent workers in the far and distant mission field sacrificially serving others. Some express their love for God through music as singers, choir members, or musicians. Some teach Bible studies, while others have gifts to create great devotionals and share deep biblical insights. Some serve on church boards or ministry committees. All have ways of expressing their love for God and their commitment to Him. It takes all kinds of kinds, doesn't it?

I believe my expression of love for God is through my knowledge of His word and through the quieter actions of meeting the needs of people. That's the way I transfer what I believe to be important. I get involved, show up, and spend time in the company of those God has placed, for whatever reason, before me.

What's your expression of your faith? Whatever it is, I bet money the impact of your expression of your commitment to God can be seen no clearer than when you are fully present, engaging in discussions, and leading by example. This all takes place through the sharing of your life, in particular with your grandchildren.

The apostle Paul might call it his *with-ness*. No matter how Paul expressed himself to many, everyone who knew him would remember how he was with people. He visited, wrote to them, and spent time with them to share with them the true reflection of a man who was touched by the hand of God.

For me, it's all about presence.

Your Presence

And I was with you in weakness and in fear and much trembling. (1 Corinthians 2:3 ESV)

I told you I recently attended the funeral of my dear friend David. I also said I walked in after the service started. I knew I was going to be late, as flight schedules just weren't working in my favor. As soon as I landed in Indy, I got a call from David's daughter asking how long it would be before I arrived at the service. They even postponed the funeral thirty minutes, awaiting my arrival.

When I arrived, I was ushered up front to sit with David's wife and two daughters. We exchanged hugs, shed tears, and held hands as we watched the celebration of a life well lived by our dear, dear loved one. We knew he had been ushered out of our presence and into the presence of God. Not much was said. Nothing needed to be spoken.

Words would have been inadequate.

Sometimes we put too much value on words. We think what we have to say is so important. We wait so anxiously to speak our minds that we miss the greater truth that it is more about who we are than about those words that come out of our mouth. Or we miss opportunities to be there for someone because we don't know what to say. Or we're too afraid we'll say the wrong thing, so we avoid someone in need. Sadly, many are convinced that words trump the presence they might have in someone's life. The desire to avoid the awkwardness and embarrassment of being tongue-tied or speechless keeps people from simply giving the gift of their presence. Sometimes one's mere presence speaks volumes.

It's your presence in your teen grandchild's life that will give you the greatest opportunities to transfer the biblical concepts you long to share.

The message of presence is greatly underrated while the effectiveness of a timely word that *sounds good* is significantly overrated. There are many situations where words don't and can't adequately convey a message of comfort, hope, or encouragement. Don't underestimate your presence in the life of your grandchild; you are *speaking* louder than you know and your grandkids are observing more than you think.

I would suggest this to you as well. It's your presence in your teen grandchild's life that will give you the greatest opportunities to transfer the biblical concepts you long to share. You may have gifts that give you an opportunity to share your faith through a number of outlets, but none are as effective as your presence in the life of your grandchildren. Just show up. Then they can spend time with you and understand who you are, not just see what you do.

Your attendance at sporting events, special events, award ceremonies and any other occasion to watch your grandchildren achieve something sends a message of value to them. Your effort to be there sends an invitation of involvement that, hopefully, will one day bring a response from that wisdom-seeking grandchild in need of counsel. When you demonstrate your *with-ness* to your grandchildren, they'll seek you out when they need trusted advice.

When you feel like just being present isn't working, you're probably not trusting that the seeds you sow into their lives will come to fruition. God promises to "complete that which He has started" (Philippians 1:6). It's your lack of patience in God's timing that can get in the way of His plan for your grandchild. We all feel like *It's not working!* at times when we don't see the fruits of our labor or the fruits of the labors of our grandkid's parents. In those times, remember this scripture, "Let us not become weary in doing good, for at the proper time we will reap a harvest if we do not give up" (Galatians 6:9). Between the time of planting seeds and the time of harvest, there is waiting and watching. It's a virtue called patience that helps grandparents understand and embrace the truth that sometimes you just have to let seeds grow in their own time.

During those growing times, remain patient and allow God to do His thing. If you're in your grandchild's field always churning and turning up the soil, you might keep that harvest from happening. That's pretty hard for many grandparents who feel like they are limited on their time. Out of the goodness of their heart, they keep talking and talking and talking…because they don't see or hear the immediate response to their presence. Have patience, my friend. Your presence is noted and recognized.

After my friend David's funeral service and burial of this rock of a man, we all stood around in the Indiana sun, feeling uneasy as to when to say our goodbyes. David's wife Amy didn't mention one thing about anything I shared. She didn't feel comfort or relief from her grief by any insights imparted by anyone. She did say this one thing as we all started to leave, "Thanks for being here, Mark." It was the greatest gift I could have given her and her daughters. Nothing needed to be said; words would have only ruined the message only presence could convey.

The same goes for your attendance at the activities your

grandchildren deem important. You're not there to do your thing; you're there to be involved in their thing.

Your Discussions

Your presence offers the invitation for discussion. Your discussions give an opportunity to engage your grandchild, affirm the relationship, and open the door for future discussions. You don't have to come to a conclusion at the end of every discussion. I like to leave all of mine open-ended. That gives my grandchildren reason to come back and have more discussion.

This is what they want in discussions with you. They want wisdom, even if they don't know that's what they want. They are looking for a welcoming place where they can discuss what they think, even if it's pure craziness and counter to what you believe. They seek someone to listen and help them process what's floating around in their heads. They are looking for a safe place to share deep thoughts and hidden

> Your grandkids want to learn what they want to know, not what you want them to know.

feelings. Remember, don't lecture. Your grandkids want to learn what they want to know, not what you want them to know. They want to be trained, not taught.

If you're asking yourself the question, *Well, if I can't lecture then how do I engage in discussion,* here are some pointers:

1. **Ask questions.** Show interest in what they have to say by asking them to go deeper in their thoughts and share from a more personal level. Questions convey value, your attentiveness, and invite them to share their thoughts with you. Here's a few to get you started.

- Why do you think that way?
- Do you think your thoughts are in line with what you believe?
- What do your friends say about this topic?

- What do you think will be important in this matter ten years from now?
- Has something happened in your life that makes you feel this way?
- Have you always felt this way?
- Do your parents know this about you?
- Have you been afraid to share these thoughts with others?
- What do you think about…?

2. **Make comments that communicate that you are listening.** Say things or little comments that assure them you are tracking with them and hanging on every word. Those comments are short conversation affirmations to show you are focused on the responses of your grandchild. Here are some comments that I use.

- That's interesting; I never thought of it that way.
- Really?
- Wow!
- What led you to believe that?
- Do you struggle with what you're thinking?
- You're kidding me.
- That really happened?
- Then what did you say?
- How long ago did this happen?
- When did you start feeling this way?
- Are you doing okay in the midst of dealing with your feelings?

3. **Don't talk in long diatribes and sermons.** Talk in short bursts. Be prepared to ask many questions to keep the conversation going. When I interview kids on our radio program, I use this method to keep discussions moving along. When I initially ask a question, I take one word from their answer and put it into the form of the next question.

Here's an example of a conversation using this method.

Question: What's one of the biggest mistakes you made in the last month?
Answer: I **cheated** on a test.
Question: Why did you **cheat** on a test?
Answer: I thought I was going to **fail**.
Question: Why did you think you were going to **fail**?
Answer: I always **fail**.
Question: Why do you always **fail**?
Answer: School has always been **hard**.
Question: Why has school been **hard**?
Answer: People don't like me very much 'cause I'm **stupid**.
Question: Do you think you're **stupid**?
Answer: Yeah, I just **say** things that are impulsive.
Question: What kind of things do you **say**?
Answer: Mostly **mean** things.
Question: Why **mean** things?
Answer: Because most of my friends seem to be out to get me.

You can see how this conversation went from a mistake made in the past month to *my friends seem out to get me.* I call it fishing. I'm fishing for responses, and I really don't care what I catch. As long as I'm allowed to fish, I hope to cast the bait deeper and deeper and deeper, until they start sharing their hearts.

In the above conversation, I went from asking about his behavior to diving into the issues of their heart. No lecture, just discussion.

4. **Don't repeat.** Remember how I said some grandparents have the tendency to tell you what they're going to tell you, then tell you, then tell you what they told you? This conversation style is rooted in the best of intentions with a desire to pass on some good information. But saying things over and over again doesn't draw grandchildren to you. It pushes them away. Grandmas and Grandpas, say it one time and leave it alone.

Bring it up in another discussion, but not in the same one twice.

Here's why I encourage you to limit your repetitiveness. If your grandchild thinks they're going to hear the same thing over and over, they'll shut down, and all the wisdom you have to share (and which they need greatly) will never be heard. You won't be given a chance to break through to a grandchild who is deeply in need.

5. **Don't talk just to fix your grandchild.** Men like to fix things. They don't want to hear the entire problem. They just want to hear what they need to do to fix it. Grandpas beware. Your intent to fix your grandson may come across as challenging his manhood. You may unintentionally remind him that he doesn't have it all together. That's not a message any man desiring maturity wants to hear. Your intent to fix your granddaughter may just remind her she is broken, not exactly how a young lady wants to be seen.

Be careful in your discussions and deliberations. Know the importance of each as these interactions help form your grandchild's view of life and how it applies to his or her world. Formation of beliefs takes place through challenging discussion and counter discussion. So if a lecture is the only form of communication with your grandkids, future counter discussion won't happen. Don't plan discussions just to transfer what you believe. Let discussions develop over time that help them cultivate all the thoughts in their head. In the process, your beliefs will be conveyed. They will get interested in what you think when you get interested in what they think.

If you're wondering what to talk about, just watch the news one night or glance at a newspaper looking for things they heard about or are experiencing. These conversations can all begin with, "Hey, what do you think about…"

- homosexuality and the gender issue argument?
- the world of politics today?
- the legalization of marijuana?
- all the shootings in our country?

- the issue of people who are in this country illegally?
- why it's so hard to love the unlovely?
- the church you grew up in and what that means to you?
- thinking less of yourself?
- abortion and women's rights for equality?
- sex trafficking?

There's plenty to talk about if you remember you're not there for them to hear you. You are there to be able to listen to them.

Your Example

We did this…to offer ourselves as a model for you to imitate.
(2 Thessalonians 3:9)

I do things with my grandkids so I have an opportunity to speak into their lives. I want to show them what it means to flesh out not only a relationship with Christ, but also one with my wife, my kids, my friends, people I don't even know, those in authority, and those who are destitute. Perhaps the bigger reason is just to have fun together.

I don't set a goal during each time together of teaching them certain spiritual truths. The truths naturally come out as we engage in activities together. It's about helping them see examples of what all those teachings look like as they enter their teen years. They want examples. They want the word to become flesh and dwell among them. They want to see a living example of one who can apply timeless truth to the crazy culture they live in.

In your teen grandchildren's world where worth and value are based on appearance and performance, they need to see and hear real substance. It is important for them not only to hear you transfer the values you hold dear into their Christian walk, but also to see what they look like in real life. As you walk and as you talk, as you sit down together and as you travel, they need to see how you act in different situations so they can imitate a lifestyle that is attractive and fulfilling.

It's their desire to see scripture lived out in someone's life with a spirit of humility and integrity. They want to see their grandparents respond with grace and strength when life deals you health issues, tragedy, great loss, or financial struggles. They long for that bigger perspective I've mentioned more than once.

> Be an example of one who lives life well within this contrary culture.

Above all, they long for an example where people are truly known by the love they have for one another, and where judgment is left to the Father.

You're it! You were chosen before the world was created to be that example for these particular kids—your grandchildren. When you choose to fulfill this role in their lives, remember that the Christian life is more caught than taught. It's better shown than talked about.

This should be your goal in all you do: Be an example of one who lives life well within this contrary culture. Show them what Jesus looks like when they look at you. You have a presence in their lives and a legacy for them to remember because you had many, many discussions and your life was a good example in a crazy world. You're not there to lead. You're there to give them someone to follow.

Chapter 25

When Life Gives You a Mulligan: A Chance to Make it Right

Forgetting what is behind and straining toward what is ahead,
I press on toward the goal to win the prize for which God
has called me heavenward in Christ Jesus.
Philippians 3:13-14 (NIV)

In recent years I notice that I know many more of the celebrities who die each year. When year-end memorials roll around, I'm surprised at how many of them I remember. When people from *your era* start dropping right and left, a friend reminded me it's a sign your time on this earth may be coming to a close. So I decided I would just quit watching all those end-of-the-year memorials.

Country singer Rory Feek and I were sitting one time at the George Jones Memorial concert in Nashville watching all the old-timey, famous-but-aging country artists get up and sing George Jones songs as a tribute to him. It was remarkable—but not in a good way—because they didn't sound so good anymore. And it was evident they're in that season of life where gravity somewhat takes over. Rory said, "It's a reminder that we're all going to be there."

If you're reading this book, you know quite a few folks in those *in memory of* reels. Use those reminders to spur you on, not to focus on where you're headed but to determine to deposit everything you can in those you leave behind here.

Parents influence. Grandparents leave a legacy.

I encourage you to make sure the legacy you're leaving is intended to meet the needs in your grandkids' lives. Don't try to cram in activities and speeches with a goal of making sure you're remembered. That's not your priority. Your priority is to invest so many important things in the lives of your family members that they can't help but remember you every time they turn around. Make sure your motivation is about meeting needs in your family, especially when your investment is desperately needed in the life of your teen grandkids.

The beauty of grandparenting is that it gives you a do-over, a mulligan, where you get to drop the ball and take another swing. You can choose to make things right in order to highlight yourself, or you can make things right because you acknowledge you missed the mark sometimes in your own parenting years. Quite honestly, I believe one way you can love your kids is by loving their kids well.

> Parents influence.
> Grandparents
> leave a legacy.

Show your kids you are willing to do for their kids what you missed doing with them. Acknowledge where you blew it, accept responsibility, and ask them for the chance to make it right. There's something pretty cool about a second chance or another opportunity to do what you didn't do before.

What I have found is that the grandparents who leave a legacy of influence and hope for their grandchildren are usually servants. They give generously, extend grace, exude gratefulness, and desire to be involved in their family. They demonstrate genuine and authentic love for each member. History and our grandkids will judge us by the wisdom of our actions, not just our words. They are watching how we treat people, how we help others, and how we serve the Lord.

I want a do over. I desire a second chance. I want to fill in the gaps I created when I was trying to parent and survive life's challenges at the same time and felt like I didn't do either very well at times. I really do want to right some wrongs, correct some mistakes, and take the wisdom I've discovered through the years and apply it to my family.

A man I was acquainted with more than forty years ago just passed away, and as I read the tributes his grandkids wrote about him, I was amazed at how he impacted their lives. I also remembered how he impacted mine. Dave Tillack spoke into my life by reminding me to consider others more highly than myself. But he said it in a whole new way to me, one I shared with you in these pages. It bears repeating.

When you're called to be a servant, don't stoop to be a king.

That is exactly how Dave lived his life. He was a servant to all, especially to his grandkids. Their lives are forever changed because of Dave's influence. This guy did it right. He is a great example of one who has passed on a legacy of hope. If half of what was said about this man is ever said about me, then I will leave twice the legacy of influence I ever thought I could.

People will forget how you look, but they won't forget how you made them feel.

Dave's impact ran deep, but it didn't develop overnight. I first met Dave and his wife Sue forty years ago when I was a young youth minister in Tulsa. Dave was forty years old at the time and wanted to teach a Sunday School class of eighth graders. I told him it was all his. His three kids grew up in the youth group and are now the dearest parents and grandparents. I know this because of the tributes they posted to their grandfather Dave. The legacy he left clearly lives on in them.

Dave's grandson Duncan is a twenty-five-year-old medical student who posted the following on Facebook:

"Grandad, thanks for making your love for everyone so clear and for always telling me that you were proud of me, even when I was doing nothing to be proud of. You told me to always know the color of my patient's eyes once I am a doctor, not just look down at the screen, and I hope I can do that. Thanks for always being so sweet to my wife Alex. I'm glad that you got to meet sweet Lively, our daughter. I'll see you again some day, but in the meantime, I'll do my best to keep making you proud. Love you."

When I spoke to Duncan, he stated his granddad was one of the most selfless people he ever met. He poured his life into others. He even joked that Grandad would wear the same clothes every day because he never thought of buying new ones for himself and would want to provide for others anyway.

A common theme that ran through my conversations with all of Dave's grandkids went a lot like this:

"He was always proud of me, and he would let you know it," Duncan said.

To Duncan, Dave was like a second dad, willing to go catch crawdads down by the creek, and always calling and catching up to find out what was going on in his life. When Dave died, Duncan shared that his granddad's life was the perfect book, and his last chapter showed everyone how to leave this earth the same way he lived.

"Grandad reconciled everything, called those he needed to call, and checked off all the boxes. I miss him dearly," Duncan said.

Grandson Tanner posted this:

"Anyone who knew my granddad knew that he was incredibly selfless and put God above and before everything else. He was always looking for ways to help and serve even if it was inconvenient or caused him pain. Looking back at the last 22 years, I can only wish I would have called him even more to hear him answer the phone with, 'Is that my sweet boy,' listened to more of his stories, appreciated his wisdom and encouragement, and asked more questions. The loss of someone you love is never easy, but to have hope in the Lord and knowing that we will all be reunited makes it that much sweeter. I pray I can be a man of God like you were and be the type of person that would make you proud. I love you, Grandad!"

Tanner told me how Dave was intentional about everything he did. He mentioned how Grandad would catch crickets and crawdads (evidently Dave had this thing for catching bugs, or was just desperate to find a way to connect with his grandkids. Ha!) What he remembers most is "how my Grandad prayed with us and for us." He said Dave wouldn't just call to ask questions, but called to be involved in their lives. Interestingly, Tanner mentioned that his Grandad was always concerned that he would one day not be relevant in others' lives. Tanner assured me that Dave remained relevant and remembered as a listener and one who constantly encouraged.

Granddaughter Caroline, a senior in high school, told me this:

"My Grandad wasn't like someone who just stopped in twice a year and gave us gifts. He knew about everything and would pray for us and celebrate with us in any accomplishment we attained," she said. "He adapted himself to my circumstances, even taught me how to serve overhand, and was one time my cheerleading coach. Can you believe that? My Grandad, teaching cheers to a bunch of girls and showing us how to build a pyramid! As clueless as he was about cheerleading, he was so determined to have an impact on each our lives. He was clueless, but wanted to have a role in your life."

She added that he had a *blunt love,* telling her once, "Caroline, you don't have to play basketball. You're not good at it." She mentioned that he never wanted to be a burden to any of them and would always say at the end of a phone call, "Okay, I'll let you get back to your life."

"He would always tell me how proud he was of me. I was there when he took his last breath and I wanted him to know how proud I was of him, having such an impact on so many people and now dying without any regrets or anybody to reconcile with," Caroline said.

Dave's college grandson Keaton said a memorable time he had with Grandad centered around handing him tools to finish out a basement in their new home.

"Grandad said, 'You're the anticipator, always handing me what I needed before I knew I did.' That was important to me," Keaton said.

He, too, mentioned that his Grandad was blunt. Dave wasn't shy about saying things that needed to be said, but always with a laugh and smile on his face.

Granddaughter Abigail wrote this on her Facebook post:

"Rest in peace to the best grandfather I ever could have asked for. No words can describe how much I love you and how grateful I am for the many things you taught me and the love you gave me. I thank God He gave me these past 20 years full of memories that will last me the rest of my life. You were such a huge part of my world. See you soon, handsome."

Another granddaughter Katie wrote,

"Today I lost my Grandad. He brought me into his arms when I was trying so hard to push everyone away. He always knew my potential and pushed me when I thought everything was too far out of reach. He gave me unconditional love and only ever judged me for my hair color. I miss both of my grandparents, but I am so thankful to meet people every day who love them as much as I do. I hope to carry that love and guidance with me every day so their legacy can live on through me."

Granddaughter Emily wrote,

"Miss you, my sweet boy. I can't wait to live my life serving others like you. Thank you for being my most loving, patient listening ear. I will forever miss your perfect answers to my endless questions. I'll be seeing you, xoxo."

Dave played a unique role in each of his grandkids' lives, always adapting new strategies to make deeper connections. If that meant getting down in the mud catching crawdads and crickets or waving pom poms coaching a handful of cheerleaders, Dave engaged eagerly and did anything to make a connection. Now when the grandkids think of how he connected, they remember the life and impact Grandad had on each of their lives. Whether they lived in the same city or were spread out a thousand miles away, Dave connected with his grandkids and left a big legacy of influence and hope.

Your Role

You have a choice. Your role, should you decide to accept it, is to offer help and hope to your grandkids at a time when they need you the most. Some grandparents choose not to. There are folks who visit every year and bring a few presents but are never known for anything much. When they're gone, they'll be described as *good people*, and that's about it. Their impact is negligible; their legacy is non-existent. Most importantly, their grandkids miss out on something they can receive nowhere else.

You have a place in their life, even if you are as old as dirt. My encouragement is not to save the best for last. Start spending yourself now. If you don't feel like you connect with your grandkids, then love yourself into their lives by the way you listen, respond, and understand.

God has you in their lives for a reason. Find out what that is and make it happen.

Your Presence

No matter how much distance there is between you and your grandchildren, you can still leave a legacy of presence in their lives. Technology makes it easy to stay in touch. Get your grandkids to set up FaceTime or Skype on your computer, tablet, or Smartphone. Don't be afraid to call, learn to text, or video call your grandkids anytime. When you know they're coming to see you, create an environment where rest and refreshment reign. Continue to love them when they're at their lowest. Invite them to be part of your life, and let them know you are interested in theirs.

Even if you are having health issues, you can still share a very important part of life with them. Your gray hair means something to them, so take advantage of it. There are very few people involved in the lives of your grandchildren that can offer them the wisdom and insight you can. That will only happen through your presence in their lives.

Your Words

The words you speak are an expression of who you are. Truly, out of the abundance of the heart the mouth speaks. What's in your heart for your grandkids? I hope it's love and acceptance, not criticism and judgment. Now, you don't have to like their attitudes or actions sometimes. But try not to let on. They get enough of that from others. Your words have the power to destroy, ridicule, demean, and crush. Or your words can encourage, support, uplift, and affirm. Be careful with your words, for they can be like a rudder that determines the direction and the ultimate destination of a great ship. Misspent words can always be forgiven, but are rarely forgotten.

Make your grandchildren proud to be yours. Lift the spirits of your grandchildren when life is weighing them down. You can speak wisdom into the life of your grandchildren or allow them to fend for themselves in a world of information that will never really give them what they desperately desire.

> Misspent words can always be forgiven, but are rarely forgotten.

Your Actions

What you do to engage with a grandchild will confirm or nullify the words you speak to them. Actions do speak louder than words, and the challenge for every grandparent is to make sure the words from your mouth match the actions others see in your life.

You can draw grandchildren to you by showing a spirit of gratefulness for your life and their place in it. You can push them away by complaining about where God has placed you. Know you are always being watched by eyes and heard by ears that will one day emulate what they see and put into practice what they hear.

Your Legacy

A great legacy is the result of a life well lived. The legacy you leave for your grandchildren has got to be intentional. You can be the greatest person ever to all your friends and acquaintances, but that doesn't matter if you fail your own family, especially your grandchildren. Take advantage of this unique relationship and be an irreplaceable lifeline to your grandkids. You can change the destiny of your family.

Another dear friend, James MacDonald, made a comment to me in passing (not the death kind of passing) that I immediately asked him to repeat. He was describing what their church, Harvest Bible Church, desired to be known for. His statement is a good one for every grandparent.

"To love without condition, welcome without judgment, and forgive without limits," James stated.

What will grandkids remember you for? Your chocolate cake? Your criticism of the culture? How clean and uncomfortable your house was? Your negativity and ability to argue? Your love of scripture but hate for mankind?

Or will they remember how warm and welcoming you were? The way you handed them the control of every conversation because you wanted to hear their hearts? Those special experiences where you laughed out loud and had fun together? The times that you just happened to show up when they needed you the most?

Take advantage of this unique relationship and be an irreplaceable lifeline to your grandkids.

How will they remember you? Will they remember what you left in their bank accounts or what you deposited in their lives? There's a big difference between what is written on your tombstone and the legacy you write on the souls of your grandkids.

My prayer for you is that when you close this book, you'll have some new ways to make memories and great reminders of how you should engage with your grandkids. As you put these tools to work in your family, your grandchildren will remember the preciousness of the time you spent with them. They'll recall the special relationship they've had with you, and how you gave them a taste of the character of God and the grace and hope He offers all His children (and grandchildren).

Your presence, your words, and your actions all work together to fulfill your role in creating a legacy of influence that will forever impact future generations of your family. That legacy will determine how you will be remembered by those who love you dearly.

May you walk with humility, demonstrate kindness by your actions, and love when you want to walk away. I guarantee if you do, you will make an impact on your grandkids and give them a lasting legacy of influence and hope.

Endnotes

Chapter 3 – How to Give Big-Picture Perspective to Your Grandchild's World

Sax, Leonard. *The collapse of parenting: how we hurt our kids when we treat them like grown-ups.* New York: Basic Books, 2017, p. 198.

Chapter 4 – A Grandparent's Greatest Challenge

Peter the Hermit quotes. Quoteland. http://www.quoteland.com/author/Peter-the-Hermit-Quotes/1599/.

Chapter 9 – How a Place of Retreat Becomes a Haven of Rest

Lewis, C. S. *The four loves.* 1960 ed. New York: HarperOne, an imprint of Harper Collins Publishers, 2017. Print.

Chapter 13 – Since Nagging and Lecturing Don't Work, Try Something Different

"nag." *en.OxfordDictionaries.com.* Oxford Dictionaries, 2017. Web 8 July, 2017.

"nagging." *Merriam-Webster.com.* Merriam-Webster, 2017. Web. 8 July, 2017.

Chapter 14 – Not Every Argument Needs to Be Argued

"Rick Warren > Quotes > Quotable Quote." *Goodreads.* https://www.goodreads.com/quotes/601712-our-culture-has-accepted-two-huge-lies-the-first-is.

Chapter 17 – Can Everyone Just Laugh a Little?

Swindoll, Charles R. "Having Fun." *Today's Insight with Chuck Swindoll.* Christianity.com. 10 Feb, 2015.

Swindoll, Charles R. *The Finishing Touch / Becoming God's Masterpiece.* Dallas, TX: World Pub., 1994. Print.

Kataria, Madan, (Kataria,1955). "I have not seen anyone dying of Laughter, but I know millions who are dying because they are not Laughing." 5 Jun, 2010. Tweet.

About the Author

Mark and Jan Gregston began their work with teens forty years ago, when Mark was a youth minister at First Methodist Church in Tulsa, Oklahoma. Their involvement with Young Life moved them to open their home to work with those who were struggling through family crises. During the 1980s, while living at Kanakuk Kamp in Branson, Missouri, Mark served as the area director for Young Life.

In 1989, Mark and Jan moved with their two children, Adam and Melissa, to Hallsville, Texas. Here they started Heartlight, a residential counseling center for struggling teens and families in crisis. To date, more than three thousand kids have resided in the Heartlight program, located in the beautiful piney woods of East Texas.

Believing that relationships create an arena for change, Mark and Jan share their lives through retreats, speaking engagements, counseling, national radio program *Parenting Today's Teens with Mark Gregston*, and the Heartlight residential program.

Mark travels most weekends, speaking or leading parenting seminars in cities across North America. He is also the proud grandfather of four: Maile, Macie, Chase, and Carter.

For more information, visit www.HeartlightMinistries.org
and www.ParentingTodaysTeens.org.

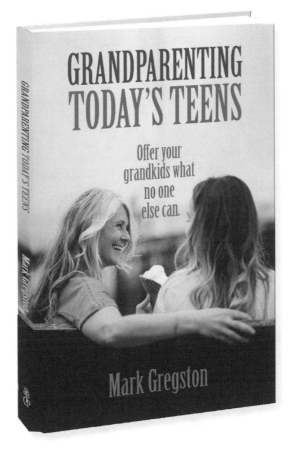

To order more copies of

GRANDPARENTING
TODAY'S TEENS

Order online at:

- www.HeartlightMinistries.org/resources
- or call 1-866-700-FAMILY (3264)

*Also available on Amazon.com
or ChristianBook.com*

Endorsements

"Mark refuses to pull any punches or sidestep any difficult situation. He speaks directly to the issues."

Joe White, Kanakuk Kamps

"These are tough times for teenagers, and Mark offers a rare blend or humor, heart and biblical wisdom."

Dr. John Trent, Gary D. Chapman Chair of Marriage
and Family Ministry and Therapy, Moody Theological
Seminary and President of StrongFamilies.com

"Mark's ministry overflows with Biblical wisdom and practical insights gained over three decades."

Dr. James MacDonald, Walk in the Word

"God has given Mark the gift to be able to speak real language to people."

Kirk Cameron, Actor & Producer

Endorsements

"This guy knows what he is talking about..."

Chuck Swindoll, Insight for Living

"Mark shares his secrets to survival and success
in raising teenagers, offering parents a hand
as they struggle for help."

Steve Largent, Former U.S. Congressman
and Member of Pro Football Hall of Fame

"Mark has a clear 'big picture' grasp of
effective parenting. It is formatted by the
power of God's grace and seasoned from
decades of experience.

Dr. Tim Kimmel, Speaker, Author, President of Family Matters

Offering **help** and **hope**
to parents and teens
in a broken world.

For nearly 30 years we've provided a safe haven for positive change. Our 9–12 month residential counseling program offers struggling teens a relational atmosphere to develop healthier patterns during their most troubling times. We've fully invested in our campus facilities in East Texas as well as a caring staff, to more successfully create lasting change in the lives of teens.

For more information about admissions, please visit heartlightministries.org, call 903-668-2173.

♡ heartlight

1,600+ stations. 1 message.

Better parenting starts now.

To find a station near you or to download the Parenting Today's Teens app visit **ParentingTodaysTeens.org**.

Real. Relevant.
Resources.

Our resources offer knowledge and perspective on today's toughest issues facing parents and their teens. This perspective comes in many forms, including books, DVDs, workbooks, curriculum, and more. Together, they compose a comprehensive foundation of knowledge and understanding. Use them for your own parenting jouney, or pass them onto a family that's struggling – it could be the very thing that turns everything around.

Visit heartlightministries.org/resources to see these resources—and many more.

WHEN IT COMES TO CRISIS,
THREE DAYS CAN CHANGE EVERYTHING.

Are you in the middle of a family crisis? Know a family that is? Our Families in Crisis Conference offers hope for a better future. This three-day conference is taught and hosted by Mark Gregston, Founder and Executive Director of Heartlight Ministries and host of Parenting Today's Teens. Parents who attend will leave with a more complete understanding of how to influence real change and help lost teens find their way back on track.

The event is held on the beautiful Heartlight campus, about 150 miles east of Dallas, Texas. **To learn more and register visit FamiliesInCrisisConference.com or call 903.668.2173.**

FAMILIES IN CRISIS
CONFERENCE

Facing a family crisis?
Call on us.

Our Family Crisis Coaching Program gives parents the opportunity to speak directly with counseling professionals—also known as our Crisis Coaches. Over the phone, from wherever you're located, they'll assess your family's situation, coach you on how to handle it, and offer proven parenting techniques.

All of our coaches have in-depth experience in dealing with teens and families in crisis. Each one holds a Masters in counseling and work or have worked with families at Heartlight, our residential counseling center for struggling teens.

If you're in a crisis, don't wait-help and hope is just a phone call away.

Sign up at HeartlightMinistries.org/CrisisCoaching or call 1.866.700.3264.

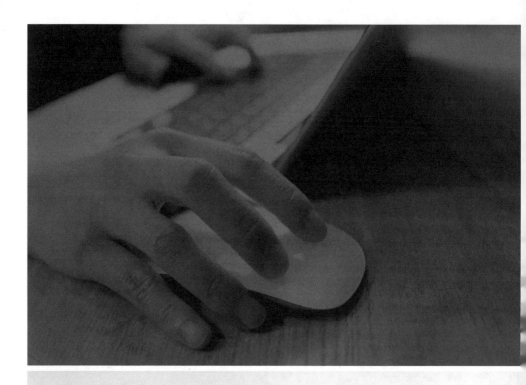

Hope. Help.
Headed To Your Inbox.